Penance: The Once and Future Sacrament

PENANCE
THE ONCE AND FUTURE SACRAMENT

Lawrence E. Mick

THE LITURGICAL PRESS
COLLEGEVILLE, MINNESOTA

THE LITURGICAL PRESS
Collegeville, Minnesota 56321

Nihil obstat: Robert C. Harren, J.C.L., *Censor deputatus.*
Imprimatur: ✢ Jerome Hanus, O.S.B., Bishop of St. Cloud, October 3, 1987.

Cover design by Joshua Jeide, O.S.B.

Printed in the United States of America.

Library of Congress Cataloging-in-Publication Data
Mick, Lawrence E.
    Penance : the once and future sacrament.
    1. Penance. I. Title.
BX2260.M53   1987   234'.166   87-29314
ISBN 0-8146-1573-2

TO MY PARENTS AND BROTHERS AND SISTERS,
who first taught me about forgiveness and reconciliation

Contents

Preface

Some seeds take a long time to germinate. Some ideas take a long time to be born. The idea for this book has been living inside me for at least six years, struggling to take form. Until now it has not been sufficiently formed to see the light of day, and as I begin the task of bringing it to birth, I suspect it may require a long and painful labor. I hope that the result will be worth the pain; only the reader will be able to make that judgment.

The seed was planted initially by the work of a study group of the North American Academy of Liturgy, which for several years attempted to probe the meaning of the sacrament of penance. The study group had agreed several times to produce a document that could be published to make its work available to a wider audience, but for a variety of reasons that goal was never accomplished.

The seed was nurtured by pastoral experience, both with the sacrament of penance and with the Rite of Christian Initiation of Adults (RCIA). Celebrating penance brings two experiences regularly: a frustration that so many people still seem to approach the sacrament in a stunted, fearful, and even infantile manner, and a joy in some cases when a person truly enters into the depths the sacrament has to offer, most often during retreats. At the same time, work with catechumens in the RCIA has constantly focused attention on the dynamics of the conversion experience, which is as fundamental to the sacrament of penance as it is to the sacraments of initiation in the catechumenate.

After a dozen years of experience in and reflection on both of those areas, I have become convinced that most attempts that have been made so far, whether by the Vatican or by local dioceses, to renew the sacrament of penance have been too narrow or too shallow to lead to a viable understanding of this sacrament. What is needed, it seems to me, is a broader and deeper understanding of the conversion process as the basis and goal of the whole Christian way of life. Only when a strong sense of conversion is deeply integrated into the consciousness of the Christian people will penance be seen as an important part of the spiritual journey of every member of the Church. Attempts to revive the sacrament by a return to the concepts and practices of recent decades seem to me to be doomed to failure. A much more radical approach is needed, in the original sense of "radical"—we need to return to our roots (*radices* in Latin). Only if we recover the richness of the Church's long tradition of conversion and penance in the midst of the Christian community can we achieve a healthy understanding of this sacrament for our own time.

Tackling this subject makes one feel a bit like the little bird that was lying on its back in the middle of the road with its feet up in the air. A fox happened along the same road and was intrigued by the bird. "Why are you lying there in the middle of the road?" the fox asked.

"I have heard a very reliable prediction," answered the bird, "that the sky is going to fall today, so I am going to hold it up with my feet."

"Oh you are, are you?" laughed the fox. "Do you really think a little bird like you, with those tiny legs, can hold up the whole sky?"

"One does what one can," responded the bird, "one does what one can!"

This little book will not solve the problems surrounding the sacrament of penance. That would be too much to expect from any one effort. But perhaps it can nudge us along in the right direction. And perhaps it will help its readers to deepen their own understanding of the sacrament and begin to approach it in a way that will be conducive to their own spiritual growth and conversion. If it does that much, it will be worth the agony of bringing it into the world.

Chapter 1

A Look to the Past

The sacrament of penance has a very interesting and varied history. Many Catholics, raised with an image of an unchanging Church, have assumed that penance has always been celebrated as it has been experienced in the twentieth century. One wit has noted that many seem to believe that Jesus and Joseph, being carpenters, must have built the first confessionals! The facts, of course, are much different, and an examination of the history of penance can be very helpful in deepening our understanding of the sacrament as well as discovering possibilities for its future.

The Early Years

The beginnings of the sacrament of penance, as with most facets of early Church life, are less clear than we would wish. Early documents are few, and concrete evidence is scarce. The Church has traditionally seen the scriptural basis for this sacrament in the resurrection appearance of Jesus to the disciples which is recorded in the twentieth chapter of John's Gospel:

> On the evening of that first day of the week, even though the disciples had locked the doors of the place where they were for fear of the Jews, Jesus came and stood before them. "Peace be with you," he said. When he had said this, he showed them

his hands and his side. At the sight of the Lord the disciples
rejoiced. "Peace be with you," he said again.
"As the Father has sent me,
so I send you."
Then he breathed on them and said:
"Receive the Holy Spirit.
If you forgive people's sins,
they are forgiven them;
if you hold them bound,
they are held bound."

(John 20:19-23)

This passage certainly seems to fit a healthy notion of penance with its emphasis on the peace Christ offers and its talk
of forgiveness. Yet Scripture scholars insist that the passage
refers, in the first instance at least, to baptism rather than penance. Baptism is the premier sacrament of forgiveness—our
sins are forgiven through our incorporation into the death and
resurrection of Christ. It is in baptism that we receive the Holy
Spirit, and admission to the Christian community through baptism requires acceptance by the community; hence sins are forgiven or held bound by the decision to baptize or to withhold
initiation.

It is perhaps not wise, however, to pose the question in
a way that assumes that the passage must refer either to baptism or to penance. Penance flows from baptism as the way
the Church deals with post-baptismal sin. Both sacraments deal
with forgiveness and reconciliation—one for those being initiated into the community, and the other for those who are
already members of the Church. It is clear that repentance and
the forgiveness of sins are at the center of the preaching of
Jesus. Conversion is the central call of the gospel, and both
baptism and penance celebrate that conversion process in different circumstances.

Later New Testament writings, like James 5:14-16 and 1 John 1:9, speak of confession of sins, and many passages call for repentance by Church members who have sinned. Yet there is almost no indication of how that repentance was expressed or how reconciliation was celebrated. Other documents from the second century indicate that the Church held to an ideal that baptized Christians had put sin to death when they went into the tomb with Christ in the baptismal waters; therefore sin should no longer have had any hold on them. Sin was part of the old life they had left behind. "How can we who died to sin go on living in it?" Paul had asked. "This we know: our old self was crucified with [Christ] so that the sinful body might be destroyed and we might be slaves to sin no longer . . . . you must consider yourselves dead to sin but alive for God in Christ Jesus" (Rom 6:2, 6, 11). At the same time, we find constant references to the Church's power to forgive sin, after baptism as well as through the baptismal death and rising.

What those early documents reveal is a tension that will persist throughout the history of penance, even to the present day. On the one hand, the Church is certain of its power to forgive, and the words of Christ insist that forgiveness by the Church is matched by divine forgiveness. The Church seeks to show the merciful love of God to the sinner and to celebrate reconciliation with the community as the effective symbol of reconciliation with God. On the other hand, the Church seeks to uphold the ideal of holiness in which sin is not accepted as a normal part of the Christian life. If forgiveness seems to be too easily available, Christians may not take sin seriously enough. There is need for a true conversion of life before reconciliation is celebrated, lest the whole process become shallow and the ritual meaningless.

In the early Church that sense of the importance of conversion naturally led to an understanding of penance as "second baptism." The first baptism was one of water, the early writers say, and the second one a baptism of tears. Just as a person joining the community through baptism had to first undergo a conversion of heart and of life, so one who had broken the baptismal vows by sinning was expected to manifest a reconversion of heart and of life before being readmitted to full membership in the community of faith.

The Catechumenate

Since the needs were similar, it was natural that the process of reconciliation was modeled on the process of initial conversion and initiation into the Church. By the third century that initiation process had developed into a somewhat standard structure known as the catechumenate. Understanding the catechumenate and the dynamics of conversion it seeks to foster can provide a solid basis for understanding the sacrament of penance.

Those who desired to become Christians in those early centuries would be presented to the Church by sponsors, who would vouch for their good character and attest that they would make good candidates for initiation. The candidates would be examined as to their intentions and their state of life. Hippolytus, in his *Apostolic Tradition* (ca. 215 A.D.), lists a large number of occupations that were not acceptable. If the candidate was a procurer of prostitutes, a sculptor who made idols, an actor, a charioteer or wrestler, a gladiator, a soldier who put people to death, a city magistrate, a sorcerer or fortuneteller, Hippolytus insists that he or she had to give up such activity or be sent away. Any occupation or activity that was in any way contrary to the Church's understanding of the gospel way of life was simply not acceptable. A conversion of life often meant a change of occupation as well as a renouncing of sin.

Once the candidates were accepted into the catechumenate, they were considered members of the community of faith, though they were not yet admitted to the sacraments. They formed a separate order in the Church called the order of catechumens, in contrast to the baptized, who formed the order of the faithful. They entered a period of formation and instruction that generally lasted three years. During that time they listened to the Word of God, attending the Sunday liturgy with the baptized until after the homily, when they were dismissed. They were instructed in the faith and its demands, and they were expected to live the Christian way in all aspects of their lives. They joined with the baptized in works of charity and service to those in need and spent time in prayer and reflection on the Scriptures.

When it was agreed that the candidates were ready to be admitted to the sacraments, they entered a period of intensive spiritual preparation lasting forty days and leading to the celebration of the initiation sacraments at Easter. This was a period devoted to prayer and fasting, and it was marked by the celebration of the "scrutinies," special rituals in which the community prayed for the catechumens that they would overcome the evil that remained in their lives and strengthen the good that was there. As the community offered support to the candidates during this period of purification, joining them in fasting and prayer and renewing their own baptismal commitment in the process, this period developed into what we know as Lent.

The period of purification or enlightenment culminated in the celebration of the sacraments of initiation at the Easter Vigil. While the community of the faithful prayed and listened to the reading of the Scriptures, the candidates were taken to the baptistery (usually a place separate from the main assembly). There they renounced Satan and pledged their lives to

Christ. Stripped of their garments, they were immersed three times in a pool of water and were clothed in white garments as they emerged from the watery tomb into new life in Christ. When they returned to the full assembly, the bishop laid hands on them, usually anointing them with oil (what we now call confirmation), and welcomed them to the celebration of the Easter Eucharist as new members of the order of the faithful.

After receiving the Easter sacraments, the new Christians continued their formation throughout the fifty days of Easter, reflecting on their experience of the sacraments of initiation and being fully integrated into the order of the faithful. Their formation would conclude with the celebration of Pentecost. (It should be noted that this description of the catechumenate is a general one; details of the formation process varied in different places and different centuries, but this description gives a good overview of the process.)

The whole point of that extended and complex formation process was to ensure that those who were initiated were undergoing a true conversion of heart and life to Christ. The call of Christ was addressed to everyone, but only those who responded to that call could be initiated into the community of the Church. The call was a call to a change of heart and a conversion of life, so the Church sought to ensure that this was occurring in the lives of the candidates before they celebrated the sacraments of initiation. Those sacraments celebrated the process of conversion that was happening, so the celebration would have been meaningless without a conversion.

The Order of Penitents

Those who had been initiated into the Church but had not lived up to the way of life that such initiation implied needed to experience conversion a second time. Since penance was seen as a kind of "second baptism," it was modeled on the catechumenate process and linked to the Lenten period. The order of penitents, as it was known, was similar in shape and purpose to the order of catechumens. Like the catechumens, the penitents entered into a unique order in the Church. The entry into that order was symbolized by the imposition of ashes at the beginning of Lent. Originally this was only for the penitents; later all the members of the community began to receive ashes as a reminder of their own need to repent.

Like the catechumens, the penitents had special places in church and were expected to leave the assembly after the Liturgy of the Word. They carried out whatever penance had been assigned to them after they had made their confession of sins to the bishop or his representative. The penance was designed to foster the conversion of heart and of life that was needed by the sinner. While they were in the order of penitents, they were supported by the prayer and fasting of the rest of the community. They might also have been assisted by the periodic guidance of their confessor or a spiritual director. In all those ways the community sought to make sure that a true conversion was taking place.

After the penance had been completed and the conversion was judged authentic, the penitents were reconciled with the community in a public ceremony, often on Holy Thursday. In the presence of the gathered community, the bishop would impose hands on the heads of the penitents and grant absolution. The reconciled pentitents were then readmitted to the table of the Lord, sharing in the Holy Thursday Eucharist.

Because both the carrying out of the assigned penance and the ceremony of reconciliation were done publicly, this order of penitents is often called ''public penance.'' There is little evidence, however, of public confession of sins. Generally the confession was made privately to the bishop or his delegate, who assigned the penance to be carried out before reconciliation would be celebrated. In recent centuries we have become accustomed to calling this sacrament by the name "confession," which indicates the importance attached to the confession of sins. In the early Church, however, the name was "penance," because the doing of the penance was seen as the most important part of the process, the part that ensured that a true conversion was taking place.

Perhaps the most surprising fact about penance in the early Church is that generally it could be received only once in a lifetime. That is a reflection of the Church's concern to be clear that it was not approving sin; the community felt that if it granted forgiveness over and over again, it would encourage people to take sin lightly. That would dilute the Church's life and witness before the world. Thus the discipline of penance was offered only once; if a Christian abandoned his or her baptismal commitment a second time, the situation was left up to the mercy of God. The Church did not say that such a person would not be forgiven but that the Church community could not do any more about the situation except to commend the sinner to God's mercy.

Such a restriction seems almost unbelievable to those of us who are used to frequent penance. It is helpful to note, however, that the discipline of public penance was required only for those who had failed seriously in the Christian way of life. The most common list of sins requiring entry into the order of penitents was threefold: murder, adultery, and apostasy (renouncing the true faith). Lesser sins were forgiven in other ways: personal penances, almsgiving, prayer, celebration of the Eucharist, etc. The public discipline of penance was required when people had so seriously violated the community's standards that they were seen as rejecting their baptism radically, refusing to live the gospel way of life. In a sense, that was an indication that their original conversion in the catechumenate had been inadequate; thus a second process of conversion was the appropriate way to reconciliation. One who would continue to flaunt the community's standards would appear not to be serious about conversion.

As time passed, exceptions were made to that "once only" rule, but the discipline of penance was never something to be undertaken lightly. It was a rigorous and long-term discipline (a baptism of tears), and the period of doing penance would often last for years. The Synod of Elvira (Spain), for example, at the end of the third century, required one year of penance for gambling with dice, five years for parents who married their daughter to a Jew, and lifelong penance for a consecrated virgin who broke her vows once. While those penances may have been unusually severe, they still give some idea of the demands of the discipline of penance. It is not surprising, then, that people put off entering the order of penitents until late in life. In fact, we find evidence that priests and bishops even advised young people not to enter this discipline too soon. They were advised to wait until they had settled down and passed the passions of youth, lest, having been reconciled once, they should fall into serious sin again and the Church would be unable to help them. Gradually penance came to be seen generally as a deathbed experience. Some people also began putting off baptism, remaining catechumens until late in life, since baptism offered forgiveness without the rigors of the order of penitents.

After sinners had been reconciled through the discipline of penance, they remained in an inferior position in the Church. They could not be admitted to the clergy or to many public offices, and they were generally forbidden to engage in sexual intercourse for the rest of their lives. Thus, entering the order of penitents was similar to what we know as entering a monastery or convent, and in time some people began to enter the order of penitents as a path to greater holiness, even though they had not committed sins which required that discipline.

The Irish Revolution

Even with those additional voluntary penitents, however, the celebration of public penance became increasingly rare. By the sixth century it was clearly inadequate to deal with the need for forgiveness of most of the Church. At this same time a different practice of penance was being carried to the Continent by Irish monks. The Irish Church, generally isolated from the rest of the Church because of the difficulty of travel across the turbulent Irish Sea, developed its own customs. The Irish did not know of the once-in-a-lifetime public penance. The Irish Church was organized around the monasteries, and the abbots functioned much like bishops. It is likely that the monastic practice of telling one's faults to the abbot or to a spiritual director led to the development of a private form of penance. As the Irish monks came to the Continent to Christianize the pagan tribes of northern Europe, they brought their penitential practices with them. In their form of penance, confession and assignment of the penance were handled simply between the priest and the penitent. This form of penance could be received as often as needed, and it did not involve any permanent inferior status.

The monks also brought with them the penitential books, which listed the penances appropriate for various sins. These books were especially helpful to largely uneducated priests, who could determine the penances simply by looking them up. Of course, if a person was a frequent sinner, it would be possible to accumulate a long list of penances, and these penances were not much lighter than those of the order of penitents. With enough sins, one could easily find it impossible to complete the penances in a lifetime, so substitutions developed. Instead of a lengthy penance, a more intense but briefer penance could be substituted. Sometimes prayers that had special popularity were substituted for a period of penance; this practice led eventually to the development of indulgences, with certain prayers or devotional practices being listed as substitutes for so many days of public penance (*not* so many days in purgatory, as many have wrongly understood).

Scholars suggest that this Irish celebration of the sacrament of penance did not originally have any form of absolution or act of reconciliation. After it became popular on the Continent, however, Church officials added a ritual act of reconciliation or absolution. For several centuries after the introduction of the Irish private penance, the bishops in local synods tried to maintain the discipline of public penance as well. Soon the general rule became that public penance was required for public sins, while private penance was allowed for private sins. That two-track system lasted for a time, but eventually the public discipline was totally abandoned in favor of private penance for all penitents.

The introduction of private penance led eventually to a change in the traditional order of the elements of the sacrament. In the order of penitents the confession was followed by the doing of the penance, which was to be completed before the absolution was granted and reconciliation achieved. With private penance the confessor also gave the absolution (rather than the bishop on Holy Thursday). Initially the penitent was still expected to complete the penance first and then return for absolution, but soon practical difficulties, such as returning to an itinerant preacher, led to the practice of giving absolution based on the penitent's promise to do the penance afterward. Thus the order became confession, absolution, and then the doing of the penance.

Since the penance was now done privately and was often shortened by substitutions, more and more emphasis began to be put on the confession of sins as an act of penance in itself. Accusing oneself before the priest came to be seen as a sign of repentance and conversion, and the penance was seen more and more as a way of atoning to God for sins committed rather than as a means of fostering the conversion necessary for reconciliation. With the increasing emphasis on the confession of sins, the sacrament itself began to be called "confession."

This emphasis on the importance of the confession itself as a means of repentance and forgiveness also led to a practice modern Catholics might find strange. If a priest was not available for confession, people began to confess their sins to another lay person or to several others. Though the lay person did not have the power of absolving like the priest, the sinner was considered forgiven through the desire for the sacrament and through the expiatory value of the penitential act of confessing his or her sins.

As the celebration of penance became more frequent, it was expected that a person with grave sins would confess before receiving communion. Gradually it became expected that all Christians would confess on a regular basis at certain times of the year. In 1215 the Fourth Lateran Council made confession obligatory for all Christians at least once a year if they had committed any serious sins.

Thus, by the thirteenth century penance had come to be much as we know it today. The Council of Trent in the sixteenth century added the requirement that serious sins must be confessed according to number and kind. That led to the common practice of reciting a list of sins and how many times they had been committed. The introduction of the confessional as the normal place for private confession came after this Council as a result of the reforming efforts of St. Charles Borromeo in Milan.

Twentieth-century Reforms

In our own century there have been several significant developments in the history of penance. The use of this sacrament has been heavily influenced by a movement called Jansenism. That seventeenth-century movement promoted a very rigorous spirituality, discouraged frequent communion, and urged "going to confession" before every reception of communion. At the beginning of this century, Pope Pius X strongly urged more frequent communion and moved the age of first communion from fourteen to the age of discretion, which has generally been understood as about age seven. Since the link between confession and communion was strong, first confession was also moved to age seven.

It took a long time to change the frequency of communion, with the fruition of Pope Pius X's efforts coming only in the 1950s and 1960s. At the same time, reception of the sacrament of penance also became much more frequent. The reign of Pope Pius XII, in the 1940s and 1950s, saw the most frequent use of this sacrament in the whole history of the Church. It is important for us to realize that this period, which seems normative to many in the Church today, was really an unusual period in the overall history of the sacrament of penance.

In the 1960s and 1970s the frequent use of penance began to decline rapidly. Various surveys and studies have been done to determine what caused that sudden drop. One of the most frequent reasons given has been a shift in Catholics' sense of sin. Some characterize this shift as a denial of the very reality of sin, and in some cases that may be true. But more often, it seems, the shift is a movement away from an overemphasis on sexual morality above all other moral issues, from an understanding of sin as a breaking of an absolute law or taboo, and from a purely private morality that tended to ignore areas like racism and economic injustice. Catholics have begun to understand sin in a more personal and broader way, and their prior experience of penance seems to many to be linked to the older view of morality. For many, confession was a ritual act with little relationship to spiritual growth or conversion. It was required in order to avoid the flames of hell, and it promised grace to help avoid sin in the future; yet that grace didn't seem to work, for people frequently complained of confessing the same sins over and over with little sense of growth or change.

Moreover, for many Catholics the sacrament of penance had become a rather negative experience, in which the sense of guilt was much stronger than the sense of God's mercy and forgiveness. One went to confession as a punishment rather than as a celebration. That all fit together when religion was understood primarily as a matter of following rules and earning one's way to heaven. When Catholics began to recover the traditional sense of God's love and mercy and the free gift of grace (which we can never earn by being good), the sacrament of penance ceased to make sense to many of those who had been regular penitents before the Second Vatican Council. The Council called for the revision of the rites of penance, and those revised rites were issued in 1969.

The new rites for penance consist of three forms of celebration of the sacrament. The first form, for individual confession, has often been falsely described as just the same as confession before the Council. In fact, this first form is intended to be a much richer and more personal experience. It is to include the reading of at least a short passage from Scripture reminding us of God's mercy, and it is supposed to be a time of shared conversation and prayer between the priest and penitent. The details of the ritual are less important than the overall experience that is intended. This form of the rite is designed to provide the time and opportunity to probe one's life and seek personal spiritual growth with the aid of a skilled confessor.

In contrast, the second form, which places individual reconciliation in the context of a communal penance service, does not envision the leisure to engage in any lengthy dialogue. The encounter with the confessor in this form must necessarily be brief due to the numbers involved, but this second form emphasizes the communal nature of our sins and of our reconciliation.

The third form, with general absolution, is currently restricted to unusual situations in which it is not possible to offer individual reconciliation. Even when this form is celebrated, those with serious sins are expected to seek out a confessor at a later time to confess those sins individually.

Since the revised rites have been issued and implemented, the individual celebration of the sacrament has continued to decline. Many parishes find that people will come in significant numbers to celebrate a communal penance service, with or without individual reconciliation, for Lent and Advent, while the weekly confession times bring few penitents. There have been various attempts, both local and worldwide, to encourage the use of this sacrament, but they seem to have had minimal effect. The most significant of those attempts was the international Synod of Bishops in 1983, which was devoted to the topic of reconciliation, including the sacrament of penance. The preparatory document for the Synod placed the sacrament within the context of the Church's larger mission of reconciliation in the world at large, and the bishops at the Synod called for more emphasis on the communal dimensions of the sacrament. The document issued by Pope John Paul II after the Synod (*Reconciliatio et Paenitentia*) stresses the idea of personal conversion in the celebration of penance, but it seems to have difficulty integrating that personal emphasis with the social and communal dimensions evident in the Synod discussions. So far there seems to be little result on the pastoral level from the Synod or the papal document.

DISCUSSION/REFLECTION QUESTIONS

1. Have you ever thought of baptism as the primary sacrament of forgiveness? How are penance and baptism related?
2. The early Church seemed to feel that sin should not be a part of the life of the baptized. Was that unrealistic, or have we gotten too comfortable with sin in our lives?
3. Has your parish implemented the Rite of Christian Initiation of Adults (RCIA) yet? If so, how has the experience of the catechumenate helped you understand conversion?
4. In what ways have you experienced conversion in your life? How was the call to conversion experienced? What helped you to make that change of heart and life?
5. Can you see how the order of penitents offered support in the conversion process of the penitents? What do you think about the public nature of that order?
6. What surprised you the most about the history of the sacrament of reconciliation?
7. This sacrament has been called "penance," "confession," and "reconciliation." Which name do you think best captures the meaning of this sacrament? Why?
8. How has the frequency of your celebration of this sacrament varied in your life? How do you decide when to celebrate it?
9. Has your experience of this sacrament been primarily positive or negative? What has made it so?
10. Have the revisions of the rites of penance introduced since Vatican II helped you to appreciate this sacrament better? In what ways?

Chapter 2

Gleanings from History

The value of history lies in what we can learn from it. It is futile to try to pick some ideal age in the past and re-create it today. Such historicism does not leave room for growth and development in the life of the Church. A broad grasp of history helps us to get an accurate picture of the tradition and to avoid being locked into any given period of that history, including the one in which we live. A good grasp of the history of penance allows us to glean from the tradition the basic dynamics of the reconciliation process and its fundamental components and to identify the basic issues that need to be addressed if this sacrament is to have a healthy role in our own spiritual lives.

The Communal Dimension

One of the most obvious insights history teaches us about penance is the communal dimension of this sacrament. Although this dimension is obvious when we study the history of penance, it has been hidden in recent experience of the sacrament. More than any other sacrament, penance has been seen in recent years as a very private affair, lacking any real community reference. The confession of sins and forgiveness were

matters between the sinner and God, mediated by the priest
as a representative of Christ. In contrast, the early history of
penance reveals a radically communal sacrament, in which
reconciliation with the community was the central act that symbolized and accomplished reconciliation with God.

Many people, Catholic and non-Catholic, question why one
should have to confess to a priest. Why not just confess one's
sins directly to God? The answer, as history reveals, is that one
can confess directly to God, but the priest is involved in the
sacrament precisely as the representative of the Christian community. Granted that it was a very limited sense of community for many people, the role of the priest maintained at least
a minimal sense of the fact that both sin and reconciliation
have effects on the larger community. Even the most private
sins affect the whole Body of Christ. When one part of the
body is ailing, the whole body suffers (see 1 Cor 12:26). Or
to use another image, if one member of the group fails to do
his or her part to advance the mission of the group, the whole
group suffers because its work is delayed and hindered.

Thus, while one can be forgiven by God directly, there is
still unfinished business until the breach with the community
is healed. Reconciliation with the community is the sacrament,
the visible and effective symbol, of reconciliation with the Lord.
The priest is the representative of the Christian community
and offers reconciliation with the Church; since reconciliation
with the Church is the sacrament of reconciliation with God,
the priest is also the representative of the Lord, but it is the
community role that is the most basic.

Most Catholics are quite familiar with the image of the confessor as a representative of God or Christ. That is a valid image in itself, since the sacrament does celebrate divine
forgiveness and reconciliation with the Lord. Yet it is an image that should not be seen *by* itself, because reconciliation

with God is intimately linked to reconciliation with the Church. To properly understand the sacrament, one should start with reconciliation with the community, and thus with the priest as the community's official representative, empowered to speak in the name of the Church and to offer reconciliation with the Church. Because that community is the Body of Christ and because reconciliation with the Church is an effective symbol of reconciliation with God, the priest is clearly recognized also as the representative of the Lord, precisely because he is the community's leader. In fact, it may be more helpful to remember that the whole Church is the representative of the Lord, the fundamental sacrament, the means through which the presence of Christ continues in our world. The priest, then, is a symbol of Christ because he is the leader of the community which represents the Lord and which is the very Body of Christ.

Recovering that communal dimension is one of the most important keys to a revitalized celebration of the sacrament of penance. It is part of a much larger recovery of the sense of community that pervades not only all the sacraments but the whole life of the Church. In the authentic Christian tradition, religion is never a private matter. God has entered into covenant with a people, and it is as a member of that people that each of us is redeemed and saved. That does not mean we have no individual responsibilities, but our life in Christ is fundamentally a life in community.

For that reason, sacraments are always communal realities. For a long time we have focused too exclusively on the effects of the sacrament upon the individual recipients. Sacraments are first and foremost celebrations of the community of faith. The community celebrates around one or several of its members who are a focal point for the celebration. The celebration does have effects on those focal members, but it also affects the whole community that is involved in the celebration. One of the basic principles of the reform of the liturgy decreed by the Second Vatican Council is the restoration of that communal dimension of Christian worship. The Constitution on the Liturgy states:

> Liturgical services are not private functions but are celebrations of the Church, which is the "sacrament of unity," namely, "the holy people united and arranged under their bishops." . . . It must be emphasized that rites which are meant to be celebrated in common, with the faithful present and actively participating, should as far as possible be celebrated in that way rather than by an individual and quasi-privately (nos. 26, 27).

We have seen significant progress in this area with the Eucharist and to a lesser extent with baptism and confirmation. We are beginning to see some recognition of the wider community role in holy orders and marriage and even in the anointing of the sick. With penance, too, there is some recognition of the communal dimension today in the popularity of communal penance services. The community dimension of penance, however, is much more basic than simply providing a communal prelude to a private confession, and it is that deeper sense that remains to be recovered by the Church as a whole. Reconciliation is fundamentally a communal event, and this needs to be both understood and celebrated in the sacrament of penance.

A Conversion Experience

A second insight that is evident in the history of penance is that this sacrament celebrates an experience of conversion. The tradition has always maintained some sense of that in its insistence that penance requires a firm purpose of amendment, a clear resolution not to give in to the same sins again. Yet the actual practice of the sacrament found many people confessing the same sins over and over, with little sense of any change in their lives. True conversion always involves both a change of heart and practical changes in one's life.

The experience of conversion is at the core of the gospel. Jesus went about preaching repentance and calling for people to reform their lives. The Greek word used in the Gospel for repentance is *metanoia*, which means a complete reversal, a turn-around to go in the opposite direction. It is that kind of conversion to which the Church calls all people. Those who respond to that call are expected to give up their sinful ways and live a new life in Christ. That initial conversion is celebrated in the sacraments of initiation (baptism, confirmation, and Eucharist). If the baptized slip back into their former sinful lives, then penance provides the opportunity to recover that original conversion and return to the way of the Lord. In contrast to the popular image of instantaneous conversions popularized by fundmentalist groups, true conversion takes time. It is possible, of course, to have a sudden conversion experience, but if it is to be lasting, it must take root and be nurtured over time. As the great theologian Karl Rahner put it, "I am a Christian in order to become one."

A real conversion of life must involve all dimensions of the person. It requires a growing personal relationship with God and a healthy prayer life. It calls for the adoption of gospel values and a life-style based on those values. It means insertion into a community of faith and taking responsibility for the work and life of that community. It often means breaking long-term habits of behavior and changing the attitudes and thinking which undergird that behavior. Thus conversion is, at one and the same time, a reality with spiritual, social, moral, emotional, and psychological dimensions. All those dimensions must be addressed if conversion is to be a lasting change of life.

The relation of penance to conversion is revealed clearly by the history of the order of penitents. Just as the catechumenate was designed to foster the conversion process for those entering the Christian community for the first time, so the order of penitents was designed to foster a similar process of reconversion for those who needed to be reconciled with God and the community. Penance was designed to enable the sinner to recover the fullness of the baptismal commitment, which had been forsaken for sinful ways. The fact that penance was known as "second baptism" by the Fathers of the Church indicates the degree of similarity between these two sacraments, both of which celebrate conversion of life.

It is also important to realize that these two dimensions of the sacramental experience—personal conversion and community celebration—are not in opposition to each other. Some mistakenly feel that emphasis on the communal dimension of the sacrament means a lessening of the personal dimension, with less likelihood of real conversion or spiritual growth. On the contrary, the communal and the personal are not opposed but intimately related to each other. True conversion in Christ is always a conversion in community. It is a movement away from isolation and selfishness to unity with others and loving care of others. And the community properly offers encouragement and support to the individual in the conversion process. Personal conversion and community responsibility go hand in hand.

This issue is really a basic one. It reveals how we understand ourselves and how we understand God's saving activity. Modern psychology, sociology, and philosophy all have come to realize how profoundly dependent we as individuals are on the example and support of the community for our own personal growth and development. It is in relationship to others that we become human. A colleague recently summed up the point well in a homily he entitled "One Chimpanzee Is No Chimpanzee." He told of a scientist who tried to study the development of a chimpanzee in isolation and discovered that the chimp would only learn to act and survive as a chimpanzee if it was allowed to live in a community of its species. The same is true of humans. We learn to be human by our interaction with others. We do not develop in isolation.

Theology teaches us the same point in another way. When God acts in history, God always calls individuals into community. Even when the call comes to an individual prophet or leader (e.g., Abraham, Moses, Isaiah, etc.), those individuals are called to form or serve the community. God forms a people of salvation, and it is in that communal context that individuals are graced and saved. Conversion to God's way always involves relationships to others and responsibility for others. Commitment to community is not opposed to personal conversion but is an essential part of it.

A Process over Time

A proper understanding of conversion and what it requires also reminds us that the sacrament of penance involves a process, not just a moment. Our sense of that process has been lost in recent years because the celebration of penance seemed to be the work of two or three minutes, preceded by an examination of conscience, of course, but still a brief experience of forgiveness. The earlier history of penance indicates clearly the need for a full process of conversion. The sacrament of penance is a moment within that process, a moment of celebration and a moment of focusing. But that moment can only achieve its proper effects if it is supported by a process leading up to it and a process flowing from it. The sacrament is meant to celebrate the experience of conversion that God is already working out in the life of the penitent. The celebration, in turn, is meant to lead into a further stage of that same conversion.

As a community, we are much like the man who was pulled over by a police officer and given a warning because his taillight was burned out. As he got out of the car and looked at the taillight, the driver became very upset. "Don't take it so hard," the officer said, "it's not hard to fix, and I'm just giving you a warning ticket."

"I'm not upset about the taillight," responded the man. "What worries me is what happened to my wife and my trailer!"

Like the distraught husband, the Christian community seems to have lost sight of a major part of this sacrament—the process of conversion that should both precede and follow the sacramental experience. Like him, we have only recently begun to realize what is missing.

The area in which I live is one of rich farmland, and it has a very flat terrain. When I first moved to the area, I went out for a bicycle ride one afternoon. After several miles of utterly level roads, I suddenly found myself at the end of a peninsula that extended into a lake ten miles long and three miles wide. Despite the size of the lake, the absence of even a significant rise in the road had given me no vantage point to see where I was headed. A sacrament is like the peak of a mountain. From the peak one can look back at the journey already traversed, and at the same time one can look ahead to the journey still to come. Being able to get that perspective enables a person both to rejoice in what has already occurred and to see more clearly the direction to which the Lord is calling.

In penance we celebrate the grace of God that has already begun the conversion process and the wonder of God's constant willingness to forgive. At the same time, the celebration issues a call for continuing conversion, for an ongoing response to God's gift and grace. If there is no process of conversion before the celebration, there is little to celebrate. If there is no continuing process after the celebration, it will have little effect in the life of the penitent. Like the summit of any mountain, it depends on the rest of the mountain to support it.

Frequency of Celebrating

The history of penance also sheds light on the question of how often the sacrament of penance should be celebrated in the life of a Christian. In the 1940s and 1950s it was common for spiritual writers and Church leaders to urge weekly or biweekly confession of sins. Confession was understood both as a spiritual discipline to foster growth in holiness and as a necessity to stay in the state of grace, since mortal sins were considered rather easy to commit. It was perhaps the constant threat of going to hell if one died in a state of mortal sin that led many Catholics of that era to flock regularly to the Saturday afternoon confession lines.

While that practice may well have helped many people at the time to strive for holiness and grow in faith, it clearly was not the normal pattern for the celebration of penance throughout our history. It is hard to give any kind of standard in terms of so many times a year or so many times in a lifetime. Few would argue for a return to the ancient restriction of once in a lifetime, yet it is clear that a mere routine celebration is not the goal, no matter how frequent.

The question of frequency must be decided on other grounds. The celebration of the sacrament cannot be placed on some sort of arbitrary schedule. It makes sense to celebrate when there is something to celebrate. It makes sense to celebrate penance when conversion is happening. As often as a Christian is aware of God's grace calling him or her to conversion, and as often as he or she is ready to respond to that grace, then it makes sense to celebrate the sacrament of penance. For some people that may be a relatively frequent thing; for others it may be very rare, though perhaps more dramatic when it occurs. In different periods of the same person's life, the need to celebrate this sacrament may be more or less frequent. When there is a lot of change and necessity for growth, the call of the Lord to convert and change may be more frequent. There will be more need in such periods to stop and take stock and clarify where the Lord is calling one to go. In other periods life will be more settled and stable, and in such times there may be less need to celebrate the sacrament. The question is not really a matter of a regular schedule for penance. The question is simply at what point it is appropriate to celebrate conversion in the life of each Christian.

It is also clear from the tradition that the most appropriate time for the celebration of penance is the Lenten season. While it is true that the conversion experience of individuals cannot be restricted to one season of the year, penance, like all the sacraments, is the celebration by the whole Church community of what God has done and is doing in the lives of its members. And the Church celebrates the continuing conversion and reconversion of its members every year in Lent. Lent is the time for penance because Lent is the time for baptism. Lent is the community's annual time of retreat and renewal of baptismal commitment, so penance finds its natural place there. Certainly the sacrament can be celebrated at any time of the year, and while Advent also has a natural appropriateness as a time of preparation for and anticipation of the Second Coming, Lent is clearly the premier season for the celebration of penance.

A Changing Sense of Sin

A final insight that we might glean from the history of penance is how the Church's understanding and use of this sacrament have been affected by a changing sense of sin within the Church. In the days of the early Church, when there was an understanding that sin was left behind with one's old life, there was not much sense of need for penance. When the Church endured persecution and faced the problem of dealing with those who had renounced Christ to save their lives, the need for reconciliation became more obvious. As the Church grew rapidly after the Peace of Constantine (313 A.D.), the level of commitment within the Church declined with the influx of vast numbers of people, and the need for dealing with sin after baptism increased. The development of the Irish system of private penance provided for more frequent use of the sacrament. At the same time, awareness of the communal effects of sin diminished, and so penance began to focus more and more on individual forgiveness instead of reconciliation with the community.

In our own time, the sense of sin that was current in the 1940s and 1950s emphasized the frequency of sin and saw sin as almost a normal part of the Christian life. Correspondingly, there was an understanding of regular and frequent celebration of penance as a normal part of Christian life. With the renewal of the gospel perspective fostered by the Second Vatican Council, most Catholics have come to understand sin in a different perspective. On the one hand, sin is seen as being more subtle and pervasive in our lives. That has led many Catholics to have some uncertainty about what to confess and how to confess it. It does not seem as clear as it once did that sins can be neatly listed and catalogued. On the other hand, there is a growing sense that Christians are called to live, by the grace of God, without serious sin. Many Christians do their best to live good lives and follow the gospel; while there are surely various faults that mark all our lives, sincere Christians are seldom convinced today that they are constantly living in a state of serious sin. These insights into the nature of sin and the Christian life have had a significant effect on the frequency of celebration of penance in the period since Vatican II.

The Church today faces the same tension that has marked the whole history of penance: how to celebrate the mercy of God fully while at the same time being clear that Christians must avoid sin and never take it lightly. It may well be that the current confusion about sin is simply an indication of a healthy re-examination of our understanding of sin and the meaning of the gospel way of life. It may be that Catholics are beginning to take sin much more seriously rather than assuming that it is a normal part of Christian life. If so, there is reason to hope that the sacrament of penance will find an important place in the life of the Church in the years ahead. That will depend, of course, on a continuing renewal and a deeper understanding of the meaning of this sacrament.

DISCUSSION/REFLECTION QUESTIONS

1. How aware are you of the communal dimension of sin? How have your own sins affected others?
2. Have you ever felt a need for reconciliation with the Church? Or has that dimension of reconciliation been unrecognized?
3. How much do you feel you are a real part of the Church community? What would help you to gain a better sense of the whole communal dimension of the Christian faith?
4. Does penance as a community celebration still sound strange to you? What can we do to recover a better sense of true celebration of the sacrament of reconciliation? Have communal penance services helped?

5. Has your experience of personal conversion involved a movement toward the community, a movement toward more loving and caring for others? Tell the story of that conversion experience.

6. How much time do you use in preparing to celebrate the sacrament of penance? How much effort do you make at continuing the conversion process afterward?

7. When do you celebrate the sacrament of reconciliation? When should you celebrate it?

8. How has your understanding of sin changed since the Second Vatican Council? How has that affected your approach to the sacrament of reconciliation?

Chapter 3

Essential Elements

One way to understand something is the analytical method: break it down into its component parts, examine each one separately, and then try to understand how the parts fit together. The sacrament of penance has taken many forms in its long history, but all of them contain the same three basic elements: confession of sins, doing penance, and proclaiming absolution or celebrating reconciliation.

In the course of the centuries those three elements have been arranged in different orders. In the ancient order of penitents, the order was always confession of sins, followed by the doing of the assigned penance, and concluded by reconciliation (absolution), which was granted by the bishop on Holy Thursday. After the Irish innovation became common and private penance was well established, the order changed to confession of sins, followed by absolution, granted with the promise to do the penance, and completed by the doing of the penance itself. With the third form of the sacrament in our current rites, the order is changed even further. Absolution comes first (as general absolution), followed by the doing of the penance and concluded, the Vatican insists, with confession as soon as possible whenever serious sin is involved. Thus history shows us three different orders:

Confession, penance, and absolution
Confession, absolution, and penance
Absolution, penance, and confession.

It is apparent that the order of the elements is not crucial, but the Church has generally tried to include those three elements in the celebration of the sacrament of penance, no matter what form the celebration takes. (That may not be an absolute principle, however, since the early Irish penance seems to have lacked any expression of absolution or reconciliation. Scholars do not agree about what is essential to this sacrament.) The regular inclusion of those three elements leads us to question the purpose of each. Why are they so important, and how are they different?

Confession of Sin

The personal confession of one's sins to a priest or bishop is probably the part of this sacrament that most people, Catholic and non-Catholic, recognize first as a central element. We noted earlier that the role of the ordained minister is to be the representative of the whole Church community, and thus secondarily the representative of God. The communal dimension of reconciliation is of obvious importance. But why is the confession of sins in itself important?

One answer to that question is that confessing one's sins is an act of penance in itself, an act of humiliation and self-denial that helps to overcome the effects of sin in one's life. That was the perspective that led to increased emphasis on the confession part of penance historically, which in turn led to the sacrament of penance being commonly known simply as "confession." This approach assumes, of course, that such an act of humility does in fact help overcome the effects of sin and leads to greater holiness. Certainly the accusation of self that confession involves should lead to a sense of humility, a proper sense of one's dependence on the grace of God, and an awareness of the limitations of one's ability to love as God loves.

Another approach sees the confession of sins as primarily a practical matter. If the confessor is to assign an appropriate penance, he must know what sins have been committed. That understanding of the role of confession was common in recent centuries, when penance was seen primarily as a judicial forum. The penitent was both prosecutor and defendant, accusing himself or herself before the priest, who functioned as judge. In order to hand down the correct punishment, the judge had to know the nature of the crime. While this judicial understanding of penance is no longer in vogue and the penance is not best understood as a punishment, this approach to the practical value of confession has validity. The confessor is supposed to guide the penitent along the journey of conversion, and the penance he assigns should be geared to helping the penitent overcome the particular sin or sins that currently hold him or her back from fully living the Christian life.

Perhaps the most helpful approach to understanding the role of confession today, however, focuses on the value of the personal encounter with the confessor as an aid to the conversion process. Work with catechumens preparing for baptism has indicated the vital importance of personal relationships (especially with the sponsors and the catechists) in fostering spiritual growth and conversion. In the sacrament of penance the encounter between confessor and penitent provides a powerful opportunity for personal growth. Psychologically, we human beings often benefit from verbalizing things we think we already know. Saying things aloud to another person often enables us to understand them more clearly. (That is the basis of most psychological counseling, especially in the non-directive approach.) And having that person reflect back what he or she hears can also be helpful in letting us see issues from another perspective. Moreover, a good confessor may also be able to give the penitent guidance and suggestions for spiritual growth. The whole experience of revealing oneself to another in an atmosphere of trust and confidence without being condemned (the priest is not really a judge in that sense) can be very helpful in encouraging growth and change. That may well be why the Vatican insists on confession even after general absolution, sensing that this personal encounter is important for fostering the conversion process that penance celebrates.

Doing the Penance

The doing of penance was considered the most essential part of the sacrament in the early Church. It was through the working out of the assigned penance that the conversion process was accomplished and reconciliation was achieved. With its constant concern that the second conversion (only available once after baptism) be effective and complete, the early Church stressed the doing of the penance as central. Thus the sacrament was named the sacrament of penance, and the doing of the penance was required before absolution was granted or reconciliation was celebrated. Doing the penance not only indicated the penitent's sincerity in seeking forgiveness but also fostered the conversion of heart and life necessary for reconciliation with the community.

Those who sinned after baptism apparently had not been converted thoroughly enough. They were a bit like the little boy who had fallen asleep close to the edge of the bed; during the night he fell to the floor. When his parents asked what had happened, he said, ''I don't know, but I guess I stayed too close to where I got in!'' Penitents stayed too close to where they had come into the Church, and the penance was designed to make sure they came in all the way the second time around.

In later centuries, when the penances were shorter and more emphasis was put on the confession of sins, the penance began to be understood as a punishment designed to atone for the "temporal punishment due for sin." This concept assumed that even though one's sins had been forgiven by God, there was still need to compensate somehow for one's sinfulness. The threat of eternal punishment was removed by God's forgiveness, but temporal punishment remained and had to be carried out either in purgatory or here on earth. The penance was understood to be a substitute for at least some of the punishment due.

There is a vital core of truth in that approach, even if its language and attitudes are not so helpful today. This core truth is that while sin is forgiven by God's gracious mercy and we are really unable to truly atone for our sins, the effects of sin in our lives and on our relationship with God and the community are not healed automatically by that gift of forgiveness. If we have failed to love as we should, forgiveness by God and the Church can bridge the gap we have created between ourselves and God and the Church. But our ability to love has also been damaged, and we may have developed a habit of sin that must be overcome. The kind of growth that is needed in such a case takes time, and the penance is supposed to foster that continuing growth and conversion.

It is for that reason that many priests today are suggesting penances quite different from the recent "three Our Fathers and three Hail Marys." While prayer is always an important part of the conversion process, many penances today are designed to foster growth in the precise area that the penitent indicates needs the most growth. If God is calling the penitent to conversion in a particular area of his or her life, then it is appropriate that the penance should be geared to that area and designed to support and encourage the conversion of life to which God has called that particular penitent. That calls for much greater creativity and sensitivity to the penitent on the part of the confessor. It may also be appropriate in some cases for the penitent to suggest an appropriate penance to the confessor if he or she has a good sense of the direction in which God is calling him or her.

Absolution or Reconciliation

This sacrament has been called penance and it has been called confession. The revised rites issued after the Second Vatican Council call it either the sacrament of penance or the sacrament of reconciliation. The terms "absolution" and "reconciliation" describe the same component of this sacrament from different perspectives. Absolution stresses the sense of forgiveness as something granted by God to the penitent. It is the declaration of forgiveness or, in the Eastern tradition, the prayer for forgiveness. Reconciliation stresses the result of forgiveness—the restoration of broken or damaged relationships between the penitent and the community and between the penitent and the Lord.

Whatever term is used, this element of the sacrament is the basis of celebration. One cannot really celebrate confession of sins or doing penance. What the community celebrates is the amazing gift of God's forgiveness and the power of God's grace to heal the damage done by our sins. The community gathers around the penitents and celebrates their reincorporation into the full life of the community. That reconciliation, which is the sacramental symbol in penance, is celebrated also as an effective sign of reconciliation with God.

In the early Church this rite of reconciliation was celebrated most often on Holy Thursday. It was a full public rite involving the whole Church community, with the bishop presiding. With the introduction and eventual dominance of private penance, reconciliation became less visible and less important in the Church's understanding of this sacrament. In our own time, the recent reforms of the rites for penance seek to recover the community dimension of the sacrament. Thus they also put renewed emphasis on the celebration of reconciliation, especially in the communal forms of the rite (forms two and three).

DISCUSSION/REFLECTION QUESTIONS

1. Has your approach to confessing your sins changed in recent years? In what way?
2. What value does confessing your sins have for you? Is it an act of humility and penance? Does it help the confessor guide you? Does it foster your conversion?
3. Have you ever confessed your sins to someone other than a priest or bishop? Was the experience helpful? What is the value of confessing to an ordained minister?
4. Can you think of a penance you were given in the sacrament that was especially helpful? What type of penance do you usually find most helpful?
5. Have you ever continued or repeated a penance beyond what was assigned by the confessor?
6. Have you ever suggested, or thought of suggesting, your own penance to your confessor?
7. Does the formula of reconciliation (words of absolution) help you experience God's forgiveness more deeply? If you were to write such a formula, what words would you use?
8. Have you ever celebrated reconciliation face to face? If not, why not? If so, what was the experience like?

Chapter 4

A Model for Understanding

Various scholars and pastors in recent years have begun to suggest that further changes are needed to bring about a true renewal of the sacrament of penance and that we need a new model for understanding this sacrament. Some have suggested that the ancient order of penitents could provide such a model for our own time. That form of penance is the fullest and richest celebration of penance in the history of the Church, and thus it has the potential to provide a full and rich understanding of the meaning of the sacrament. While knowledge of the history of the sacrament can provide such an understanding to those who will study it, deepening the understanding of the whole Church community will happen only through the way the Church celebrates penance today.

The possibility of reinstituting the order of penitents seemed almost unthinkable just a few years ago. In the last decade, however, many parishes have had experience with the catechumenate through the implementation of the Rite of Christian Initiation of Adults. That rite, which was issued by the Vatican in 1972, restores the ancient catechumenal preparation for adults seeking to be baptized. In the process of their formation, a process that seeks to support and foster conversion of heart and life, the catechumens come before the whole community of the faithful several times to ask their prayers and to share their conversion experience. They come before the community the first time when they are officially enrolled as catechumens, forming the order of catechumens within the Church. That ceremony takes place after they have completed a pre-catechumenate period and have decided that they definitely want to be members of the Church. From that point on, they belong to the Church, but they are not yet members of the order of the faithful, since they have not been baptized yet. Experience with this special order of non-clerical members of the Church can pave the way for understanding the order of penitents as another, similar order.

At the end of their cathechumenal formation (which may last as long as several years), the catechumens come back before the community to celebrate their call to the sacraments of initiation. This celebration usually occurs on the First Sunday of Lent, and it marks the beginning of the period of purification or enlightenment, a time of prayer and spiritual growth. During this period, which coincides with Lent, they come before the community three more times, on the Third, Fourth, and Fifth Sundays of Lent, for the celebration of the scrutinies. Scrutinies are essentially prayers by the whole community for the candidates that evil will be overcome in their lives and that what is good will be strengthened.

There was considerable concern when parishes began to introduce the Rite of Christian Initiation of Adults that this public prayer for their conversion would put the catechumens in an awkward position and lead the community to look down upon them as inferior. Experience has shown, however, that with reasonable care in preaching and explanation just the opposite occurs. The catechumens are admired because they are taking the gospel seriously, and they are respected for their willingness to share their conversion journey with the larger community. Moreover, their witness to the importance of conversion has a significant effect on the whole Church as all the faithful are reminded of their own need to be converted and to renew their baptismal commitment. That is part of the ministry of the catechumens to the community—to call the whole Church to deepen their conversion. That assumes, of course, that the community as a whole has been led to a proper understanding of conversion as an ongoing task of every Christian, not simply as a necessity for the new members of the Church.

An order of penitents within the community would likely have a similar effect, assuming a similar understanding of the importance for every Christian of continually renewing and deepening one's conversion to Christ. Through the catechumenate many parishes have become accustomed to a group of candidates for initiation who have a public role in their worship, especially in the Lenten season, when the catechumens prepare intensely for the celebration of the sacraments of initiation at Easter. Those communities have become aware of the influence on the whole community that is exerted by the witness of those who share their conversion journey with the whole Church. Many of those same communities have also found that the witness of catechumens prompts several baptized Catholics to come forward and ask for a similar opportunity to enter a conversion process with the support of the community. It is not appropriate for those who are already full members of the community to enter the catechumenate, but an order of penitents could provide just such an opportunity for deepening one's conversion.

An order of penitents today could not reasonably be limited to those who are guilty of murder, adultery, and apostasy, as it often was in the early Church. That would be more

than the Church could expect even of great sinners in our culture, for entering the order with those limitations would be
tantamount to a public confession of sins. There are three
groups that would seem to be proper candidates for an order
of penitents. The first would be those who have sinned seriously in any way and now seek to reform their lives and return
to gospel values. The second would be those who have left the
Church for a time and now desire to return to full and active
membership. Such people often note the need for some process over time that will be a true reintegration into the community's life. The third group would be those who, although
they have not sinned seriously nor left the community, still
sense a call from the Lord to deepen their conversion in some
significant way. Like those who entered the ancient order of
penitents to seek greater holiness, such modern penitents would
seek to deepen their relationship with God and their conform-
ity to Christ. The inclusion of all three of those groups in
a modern order of penitents would help avoid the labeling
of the members of the order as greater sinners than the rest
of the community. They might, in fact, be among the holiest
of the community's members.

The existence of such an order within the parish community would serve as a regular reminder to the whole Church
of the need for continual conversion. We have spoken thus
far of conversion as a process for catechumens preparing for
baptism or for penitents preparing for reconciliation. It is in
those cases that the dynamics of conversion are the most intense and complete. But conversion is also an ongoing demand
of the gospel. In a sense, the whole of Christian life is a process of conversion, continually deepening our relationship with
the Lord and conforming our lives ever more closely to the
gospel. That is ultimately the work of a lifetime, and every
member of the community is called to constantly deepen that

conversion. That is the purpose of all spiritual disciplines, of religious education, of preaching and prayer, of all that the Church does. The Christian life is a life of continual conversion, of constantly turning oneself more completely over to the Lord and conforming one's life to the gospel. The Christian community seeks such conversion at all times and in all places, but it focuses on the need for continuing conversion in a special way during the Lent-Easter cycle each year. The ministry of the catechumens and the penitents to the larger community is to be a visible, enfleshed witness of the need for that ongoing conversion.

An order of penitents could be structured in a variety of ways, and there is no absolute pattern that must be followed. Those who have suggested its re-establishment in the Church, however, usually follow the model of the ancient order of penitents to some degree. Entrance into the order would be celebrated on Ash Wednesday with the imposition of ashes, the assigning of special places in the church, and perhaps the giving of a special garb. Such penitents would, of course, have already made a confession of sins to a priest or bishop, who would have assigned the penance to be carried out in the order of penitents. That might have happened even months before if the penitent and confessor together judged that the order of penitents would be a helpful spiritual discipline for the individual at this point in his or her life. More likely it would have taken place shortly before Lent, perhaps following a special invitation from the pulpit or in the bulletin for anyone who might benefit from the experience of the order of penitents to make an appointment to speak to a confessor.

During the period of Lent the members of the order of penitents would seek to deepen their conversion in a variety of ways. They would carry out the penance they had been assigned, which would presumably be something designed to be done throughout Lent. They would meet periodically with either their confessor or another spiritual director, who would seek to guide their journey and perhaps adjust or add to their penance if it would help their growth in Christ. They would probably meet together as a group to support one another through prayer and mutual witness about what they sense God is accomplishing within them. They would ask the prayers of the whole community of the Church, both informally and during the Sunday worship as the catechumens do.

Following the example of the catechumenate, the penitents might also be dismissed after the Liturgy of the Word during the Eucharist. Thus they would abstain from receiving the Eucharist throughout the Lenten period. This proposal is worth considering, though it might entail some difficulties, even if the catechumens are dismissed at the same time. Catechumens are unbaptized and thus cannot receive communion, so their dismissal to their own assembly is quite understandable. But penitents are baptized members of the community, and some people may feel it would be a harsh punishment to deny them the Eucharist. Historically, we can find evidence of communities in which they were dismissed and others in which they were not, so both options have precedent. Current canon law assumes that members of the faithful in good standing will participate in the Sunday Eucharist, so the inclusion of those who are simply seeking a deeper conversion may make the dismissal of the penitents impractical.

If such a dismissal were implemented, it would be important to clarify that it is not so much a punishment as it is a spiritual discipline. The penitents "fast" from the Eucharist in order to symbolize concretely their special state and to heighten their desire for full reintegration into the order of the faithful. Then their readmission to the table on Holy Thursday becomes a powerful experience of renewal and reconciliation. In addition, their dismissal from the assembly of the faithful should be a dismissal to their own assembly as penitents. That would provide an opportunity for them to discuss together the application of the Word of God they have heard and how it applies to their special journey. The catechumens do a similar thing in their own assembly after leaving the larger group.

To understand the dynamics of an order of penitents or the order of catechumens, it is helpful to remember that both of these are temporary orders. The order of the faithful (the baptized) and the orders of deacon, priest, and bishop are permanent orders, but the orders of penitents and catechumens are entered precisely as a transition stage. As such, these two orders form what sociologists call "liminal states." The term "liminal" comes from the Latin for "threshold" (*limen*), and a liminal state is a transitional one. Studies of both ancient and modern liminal periods and rites of passage have taught us much about how the process of change can be fostered in the lives of individuals in a community context.

The liminal state has several common characteristics that can help us understand the dynamics of an order of penitents. The first is that those who are going through a rite of passage must leave the normal social structure. In tribal societies they leave the village and have no social role in the community during their liminal period. So, too, penitents leave their usual role as members of the faithful. They are given special places in church and perhaps special garb, and are dismissed from their normal assembly.

Second, there is a radical equality among the initiates, regardless of their previous status. In the order of penitents all penitents are equal, all seeking to deepen their conversion, and the formation of a clearly identifiable and united group is an important part of the process. Hence, time spent together as a group, special places in church, the dismissal, and whatever deepens their unity can be helpful. That equality is accompanied by a submission to a common authority. For the penitents, the authority is the Lord, who accomplishes their reconversion through grace. But there is also a submission to the guidance of the spiritual director who seeks to foster the conversion experience.

Finally, the initiates have to undergo some ordeal, some time of proving themselves, which usually involves significant self-denial. For the penitents, that is primarily the assigned penances, but the abstention from the Eucharist could also be part of it. One of the effects of the ordeal is a sense of completion and accomplishment when it is over, a sense of having reached a new position in life. So, too, the temporary denial of the Eucharist could lead to a sense of completion and reintegration when the penitents are readmitted to the table on Holy Thursday. Perhaps the future will see changes in canon law to explicitly provide for an order of penitents, just as the recent revision of the Code of canon law now provides for the order of catechumens.

The order of penitents would conclude with readmission to the table. That was traditionally celebrated most often on Holy Thursday so that the reconciled penitents could participate fully in the Easter liturgies. The main sign of reconciliation is precisely that readmission to the table of the Eucharist, but it would normally be preceded by some brief ceremony that would involve the laying on of hands and speaking the words of absolution. Such a ceremony might well focus on the gratitude due to God for the grace of conversion and forgiveness manifested in the lives of the penitents.

This model of an order of penitents is obviously less demanding than the ancient order in that it would generally last only through the six weeks of Lent rather than taking years

to work out stringent penances. Yet it still captures much of
the value of the ancient process. It is, first of all, clearly a process
of conversion over time. It draws upon the prayers and witness and support of the whole community. It challenges the
penitents to an intense spiritual journey and assists them with
spiritual guidance. It is clearly a communal experience, cul-
minating in the communal celebration of reconciliation. It provides a living witness for the whole community, calling all the
members of the Church to deepen their own conversion. And
it clearly links penance with baptism, since it parallels the conversion journey of the catechumens. In all of these ways an
order of penitents provides an important model for understanding the meaning of the sacrament of penance. It should not
be expected that many people would actually enter the order.
Even in a large parish, the number each year who would benefit
from such an intense experience would probably be small. Yet
those few, like the catechumens, are a representative group,
and their witness to the conversion process and its importance
is crucial for the larger community.

Parishes that have implemented the RCIA and developed
a healthy catechumenate have noted that people soon begin
to understand baptism in light of the adult initiation experience. That is true despite the fact that most baptisms in
those parishes are still infant baptisms. The number of catechumens is much smaller, but that experience becomes the basis
for understanding the meaning of baptism. That happens for
several reasons: the catechumenate is a richer and fuller celebration of baptism, it occurs more publicly and over a period of
time, and it involves adults, with whom other adults in the
community can easily identify. A similar pattern can be an-
ticipated with penance. Though most celebrations of the sacrament may well be outside the full order of penitents, that fuller
and more public form of penance would provide a model for

understanding the dynamics of conversion that the sacrament celebrates. It would remind all members of the Church that penance requires a process over time, that it has communal implications, that it can draw on the prayer and support of the community, and that it is always about conversion, about a true change of life.

This proposal for an order of penitents has already garnered a significant amount of support on various levels within the Church. It was proposed by a study group of the North American Academy of Liturgy as far back as 1979, and it became the focus of that group's work for several years. When the issue of reconciliation was announced as the topic for the 1983 Synod of Bishops, several members of the group contacted Cardinal Joseph Bernardin, who was one of the American representatives at the Synod. After various contacts with different members of the study group, Cardinal Bernardin adopted the approach as his own and obtained the support of the other members of the American delegation. As a result, a proposal for the re-establishment of the order of penitents was part of the American bishops' contribution to the international Synod. Though the proposal was not mentioned in the papal document after the Synod, its discussion at the Synod itself certainly lends a certain credibility to the idea.

During these same years various parishes across the country have been experimenting with an order of penitents on the pastoral level. Those experiments have been a response to perceived pastoral need, which often surfaced as a result of the catechumenate. Various people began to ask for a similar program of conversion therapy for the already baptized, and an order of penitents seemed to be the logical response. Those experiments have been successful enough to establish the practical viability of the idea; it is not just an "ivory-tower" theory but a pastorally useful proposal.

There are some who suggest that the order of penitents would be a fourth form of penance, added to the three official forms in the revised rites for this sacrament. It is also possible to see it as simply an adaptation of the forms already approved. It could well be seen as simply spreading out the first form of the sacrament (individual reconciliation) over time and adding a communal context for the celebration. Or it could be understood as the second form (communal service with individual confession) spread over time with an expanded opportunity to interact with the confessor as spiritual guide. It does not seem necessary to have explicit permission from the Vatican to implement the basics of this proposal, since it really just expands and enriches forms already approved.

This form of celebration of penance also helps us understand the idea of celebrating a sacrament from a different perspective. For too long we have focused exclusively on the ''recipients'' of the sacrament, as if their readiness and the effects of the sacrament on them were the only issues at stake. The renewal of sacramental theology since the Second Vatican Council has focused our attention more and more on the role of the whole community. It is the full community that celebrates the sacraments. The community celebrates around the individual or group that is the focal point of the celebration, but the whole community is celebrating, not just the recipients. And the whole community is affected by the celebration. In the case of penance, the whole Church celebrates penance during Lent, focusing its celebration around those who have entered the order of penitents, and the whole Church enters into the process of conversion and celebrates God's mercy reflected in the lives of the formal penitents as well as in their own lives. Perhaps that is a better model for understanding the relation between Lent and penance than assuming that every member of the community will individually celebrate the sacrament during Lent. With the decreasing number of priests, that approach may well become practically impossible, but every member can celebrate penance through the community's involvement in the order of penitents.

DISCUSSION/REFLECTION QUESTIONS

1. Does the model of the order of penitents help you to understand this sacrament better? In what ways?
2. Can you imagine having an order of penitents in your parish? How would you structure it?
3. What might be the effect of an order of penitents on your parish?
4. Do you see conversion as central to the Christian life? Do the other members of your parish see it that way?
5. Can you imagine entering an order of penitents? Can you think of other people who might find it helpful?
6. Can you think of a time when you were in a liminal period in your life? What was it like? How did you enter and leave that period?
7. How can you incorporate the values of an order of penitents into your own approach to this sacrament?

Chapter 5

Making It Personal

Of all the sacraments, penance is the most personal, for it deals with the innermost part of our selves, touching us in that realm of guilt and love that is the most intimate part of our relationship with God. It is no doubt for that reason that the renewal of this sacrament has been slow and difficult to accomplish. Change is always difficult, but it comes most slowly when it deals with such personal matters. The renewal of this sacrament requires a shift for many people in their image of God, in their understanding of sin, and in their appreciation of conversion as a way of life in Christ. With the model of the order of penitents in mind, let us now examine several issues that can help us find a way to rediscover the value of the sacrament of penance.

Salvation in Community

One of the most difficult but also most important perspectives that we need to regain in the Church is that salvation comes to us in community. At least in this country, we are such individualists that we find it difficult to think of ourselves as truly a part of a community. Our national tradition stresses the rights of the individual, and our mythology is filled with images like the Lone Ranger riding off into the sunset. Our music pleads "Don't fence me in," and we pride ourselves on self-reliance and independence ("I did it my way").

While there is certainly merit in such self-reliance, an over-emphasis on the individual has blinded many of us to the essential role of community in our personal development and in a full human life. God has never suffered from such short-sightedness. When God acted in history to bring about salvation, God chose a people. The covenant God offers us is a communal covenant, a relationship between the People of God and its Lord. It is precisely as a member of that people that we are saved. It is to be a member of that people that God calls each of us and claims us as adopted children. Certainly it is true that we have individual responsibility and that we are guilty of our own individual sins; yet there is nothing we do as individuals that does not have its effect in the community of God's people.

We have already spoken about the effect of that perspective on our understanding of sin, for even the most private sins affect the whole Body of Christ, the whole People of God. So, too, reconciliation with God must always include reconciliation with the People of God. But the consciousness of our community connection must pervade our awareness if we are to fully appreciate the sacrament of penance. Reconciliation is what salvation is all about. The work of Jesus is described in the New Testament as a work of reconciliation:

> It pleased God to make absolute fullness reside in him and, by means of him, to reconcile everything in his person, both on earth and in the heavens, making peace through the blood of his cross (Col 1:19-20).

That same mission of reconciliation is to be carried on by the Church:

> All this has been done by God, who has reconciled us to himself through Christ and has given us the ministry of reconciliation. I mean that God, in Christ, was reconciling the world to himself, not counting people's transgressions against them, and that he has entrusted the message of reconciliation to us.
>
> (2 Cor 5:18-19)

That reconciliation is not just between God and individual humans. It is also a reconciling of people and nations with one another. Paul describes it in his letter to the Ephesians in discussing the relationship between Jews and Gentiles:

> It is he who is our peace, and who made the two of us one by breaking down the barrier of hostility that kept us apart. In his own flesh he abolished the law with its commands and precepts, to create in himself one new person from us who had been two and to make peace, reconciling both of us to God in one body through his cross, which put that enmity to death.
>
> (Eph 2:14-16)

Thus the formation of a community of faith and the breaking down of barriers between people are intimately related to reconciliation with God and overcoming sin. Sin always affects our relationship with others as well as our relationship with God; hence salvation always involves both dimensions as well. Recovering a vital sense of the centrality of the community of faith in our own personal salvation would go a long way to help us recover a sense of the vital role of penance in our personal spiritual lives as well as in the life of the Church community.

For community to be real, however, there must be an atmosphere of true caring for one another. Many parishes are so large that we have learned to accept anonymity as a normal part of Church life. It should not be so. Many larger parishes have begun to subdivide into smaller groups or mini-parishes to enable the parishioners to get to know one another and to develop bonds of sharing and caring with fellow Christians.

However it is accomplished, such an atmosphere is essential to the renewal of the sacrament of penance. Parishioners need to learn to care for and pray for one another, to support one another in times of difficulty, and to share their spiritual lives together in various ways. Experience with the catechumenate suggests that an order of penitents would foster such an atmosphere, though it cannot achieve it alone. As part of an overall development of a parish's sense of reconciliation, however, it could be a significant help.

At the same time, Christians need to recognize their common situation as sinners. Some people object to the recent stress on community because they find too many things they dislike about the Church community. The Church is not all that it should be; it is imperfect and sinful. The evangelist Billy Graham once responded to that issue, saying, "You want a perfect Church? Go find a perfect Church and join it. Then it won't be perfect anymore!" We form a community naturally because we are all sinners and all in need of redemption. In Christ we form a community of sinners being redeemed through God's grace. There is no room for any attitudes of superiority or condemnation of others. Many fear implementing an order of penitents lest other parishioners look down on those who enter the order. The same fear was present when the RCIA began to be implemented, but experience has shown that it is not a major problem. In the RCIA, emphasis is placed on our common journey of conversion and our common need for God's grace. Exactly the same emphasis is needed for an order of penitents. Recognizing our common need for forgiveness was one of the salutary benefits of the old confession lines. It is also manifested in the current popularity of penance services before Christmas and Easter. With proper guidance, the same awareness can be fostered in an order of penitents.

Our Image of God

Since penance deals rather directly with our relationship with the Almighty, our image of God is a crucial issue in our approach to this sacrament. So many people express fear of this sacrament that it seems we have internalized a very negative view of the God we meet there. It may well be that such a negative image has been fostered by encounters with negative confessors, yet it is the image of God that must be revised. The older emphasis on penance as a forum for judgment no doubt contributed to that image, so it is helpful to start by rethinking why we approach the sacrament at all.

By the time we approach the sacrament of penance, generally the judgment has already been made. We have judged ourselves guilty of sin and in need of reconciliation. There is no need, really, for God or the priest to judge us, though the priest may well help us to clarify our judgment of our lives. What we seek after the judgment has been made is a word of forgiveness and an experience of reconciliation. We approach a God who has promised to be always ready to forgive and a community (represented by the priest) that is pledged to minister reconciliation. The dominant image of God in this context should be the prodigal father of the fifteenth chapter of Luke's Gospel rather than a stern judge waiting to condemn.

Of course, this issue is much broader than the sacrament of penance. Our image of God in general often owes much more to pagan ideas than to the revelation of the Father given to us by Jesus. Christianity is a radically new religion in the long history of the human race precisely in its image of God and its approach to God. Jesus revealed to us a God who invites us into intimacy with the Godhead. In contrast to the trembling pagan fearfully approaching the throne of the idol, we are invited to gather around the table of the Lord in the intimate setting of the upper room where the Last Supper was celebrated. Jesus teaches us to call God "Abba," which is closer to "Daddy" than the formal "Father." (As an exclusively male image, though natural for its time, "Abba" may not be acceptable to many women today, but we need to retain the intimacy and familiarity suggested by that name.) In short, our God has invited us into an unheard-of closeness, a relationship of family love (we are adopted children of God) that is unique in the history of world religions.

The story is told of a young boy who ran out of the crowd during a parade and jumped on the carriage of the Roman emperor. A guard rebuked him, saying, "Don't you know this is the Emperor?"

"Yes," the boy replied, "but he is also my father."

It is that kind of free access to the throne of grace that Christ has offered us. As God's adopted children, we can approach the Lord freely and intimately. It is not surprising, perhaps, that we have only begun to assimilate that radical change, for we are fighting thousands of years of pagan images that have pervaded our cultures and our consciousness. Even if we have changed our conscious image to be more in accord with the gospel, our instinctive and emotional responses may still be tied to the ancient, fearful pictures of God. Our spiritual lives in general, and our appreciation of the sacrament of penance in particular, would be helped greatly by frequent reflection on the images of God that Jesus used to reveal his Father to us. The more we learn to relate to God in intimate trust and love, the more we will come to appreciate the encounter with God in the sacrament of penance as a positive and desirable experience.

Our Understanding of Sin

Surveys done over the past couple of decades have indicated that a major reason for the decline in the use of the sacrament of penance is a shift in people's understanding of sin. There are a variety of issues that this topic encompasses, and all of them deserve our attention. Part of the shift has been a different understanding of mortal and venial sin. Part of it has been a deeper sense of social sin, especially in the areas of war and peace and injustice and poverty. And part of it has dealt with the communal dimensions of all sin, social or private.

a) From taboo to love

Underlying all these issues, however, is a shift in the practical definition of sin itself for many people. By "practical definition" I mean the understanding of sin that is actually operative in a person's life, defining both virtue and guilt, as opposed to a theoretical definition that has been memorized or that might be expressed in answer to another's questions. Regardless of what they might have said in theory, many Catholics in the recent past operated with a sense of sin that equated sinning with breaking a taboo. A taboo is an inflexible, often unreasonable law that must be observed strictly; if it is violated, punishment is automatic and inevitable. A good example from childhood is the old saying "If you step on a crack, you'll break your mother's back." How many millions of children walked to school carefully avoiding the cracks in the sidewalk? That, of course, was primarily a game, and most children didn't really believe it would happen.

In more serious moral matters, however, many Catholics viewed sin as primarily a matter of breaking the rules. No matter what the circumstances, if the rule was broken, punishment would follow. It is not uncommon even today to have older Catholics confess missing Sunday Mass, even though they were hospitalized or prevented from coming to church by bad weather. When a confessor explains that such an absence is not sinful, the common response is, "I know, Father, but I still feel better if I confess it." That's a good example of a practical definition of sin that differs from the intellectual understanding a person has. Even though they know it's not a sin, emotionally and instinctively they deal with it as sin.

That kind of taboo approach to morality is where we all begin in our understanding of sin. A small child learns not to touch the stove, not to cross the street, or not to hit the baby, because Mom or Dad establishes such behavior as taboo. No reason is needed and no excuses are accepted. Such an approach is appropriate for a toddler, but as we grow and mature our understanding of virtue and sin should change. The persistence of a taboo mentality into adulthood is really a sign of stunted moral development.

A more mature approach to morality judges actions on the basis of the beneficial or harmful effects in the life of the person and/or on others in the situation or in society at large. This approach seeks to understand the reasons an action is right or wrong rather than accepting it just as an irrational law. In this view, a sin is a sin not just because God said so but because it is bad for human growth and happiness or has negative effects on the society at large. God has revealed what is sinful in order to help us live a truly happy and fully human life. To sin is to harm oneself and others, and the punishment for the sin is largely contained in the sin itself, in the effects it has on one's growth and happiness.

This approach has much merit and is a significant advance over a taboo mentality. It reveals some very important insights into the relationship between moral behavior and human development, between virtue and personal growth and happiness. Yet it still falls short of the gospel perspective on sin and morality. It is fundamentally a humanistic approach that would make sense of itself even if there were no God in the universe.

The Scriptures, on the other hand, present sin in the context of our relationship with God. Sin destroys or harms relationships, both with God and with others. Sin is ultimately a rejection of love, a refusal to love God in response to the divine love we have received and a refusal to love others as God loves us. It is this personal and relational understanding of sin that is the truly Christian approach. It is not hard to see how that meshes with the image of God that Jesus revealed. God calls us into a relationship of love with the Trinity and with all God's people. To refuse that love is to sin. Sin damages the love relationships on which our lives should be built, and forgiveness is always a matter of reconciliation, of repairing or re-establishing those relationships.

Since Vatican II more and more Catholics have been moving toward this Christian approach to sin and virtue, and that has affected their use of the sacrament of penance. When sin is viewed as a taboo with automatic punishment, penance is understood as the way to appease the Deity and avoid the punishment. Hence it must be sought as soon as possible, and since taboos are easily and frequently broken, a frequent use of the sacrament is necessary. If sin is understood from the humanistic perspective, penance is less important, since correction of the error and resuming one's growth is all that is really required to overcome the effects of sin. But if sin is understood in the context of relationships, then penance becomes a matter of great importance, not to appease an angry God but to rebuild the love relationships that form the basis of life.

It seems likely that many Catholics have progressed only part of the way along this journey from taboo to love relationship. Such growth in moral awareness occurs only over time and is appropriated slowly. Many have, no doubt, rejected the taboo approach and moved to the humanist mentality, but they have not yet progressed to the gospel perspective that sees sin in personal terms. Thus they have abandoned penance as unnecessary, since the humanist mentality has less use for it. It will require further growth to understand sin in relational terms before the importance of the sacrament of penance as reconciliation will be appreciated.

It is also likely that many people have grown in their understanding of morality without an accompanying shift in their understanding of penance. If penance is still seen, either intellectually or instinctively, as avoiding taboo punishments, while one's understanding of sin is no longer the taboo mentality, then the value of the sacrament will not be appreciated. The development of communal penance services and the use of the name "sacrament of reconciliation" has helped many to adjust their understanding of penance to match a deeper understanding of sin and morality, but there is still a great need for a better appreciation of how penance responds to a renewed approach to morality.

b) Mortal and venial sin

In years past one of the most common questions about a sinful action was whether it was mortal or venial. That distinction has received less attention in recent years, probably because it was linked so closely to lists of sins that seem less useful today. Nevertheless, the distinction is still valid and can be a helpful one if we understand it in the perspective of the love relationship between ourselves and God. In this context a mortal sin is one that completely destroys that love relationship. Of course, God's love for us is constant, and nothing we do can destroy that. But a relationship requires two sides, and mortal sin is total rejection of that love from our side. It is, in effect, telling God to get out of our life completely.

Now it should be apparent that the average Christian is not going to commit mortal sin very often. It is a radical rupture of the bond between us and God. It cannot happen by accident, and it requires a certain degree of maturity and deliberate intent. It is not necessary, of course, to consciously reflect on the fact that we are totally rejecting God. We know, almost instinctively or because of our prior training and reflection, that certain actions are fundamentally incompatible with continuing to love God. To choose those actions is tantamount to rejecting God, because we know that we cannot choose one without rejecting the other. As a parallel, a husband normally understands that he cannot beat his wife every night and expect the relationship to last. He doesn't have to stop and consciously decide that he wants to drive her away; he knows almost without thinking that such actions will have that result. So, too, we know that mortal sin cannot coexist with an ongoing relationship with the Lord.

Venial sin, on the other hand, is a less serious, less total rejection of God's love. It damages the relationship but is not so serious that it causes a complete rupture. There is still a need for reconciliation, for the bond of love has been weakened. There is no radical break, but the relationship needs to be strengthened and reaffirmed.

It is important not to trivialize the significance of venial sin, for every sin is a tragedy in light of God's overwhelming love and goodness toward us. No Christian should ever be complacent about even the smallest sin. Moreover, venial sin can lead us toward that total rejection of God that mortal sin causes. Venial sins do not add up to a mortal sin, no matter how many they are. But repeated damage to the relationship, repeated rejections of God's love, can gradually weaken the bonds of love to the point that we might make the complete break and sever the relationship completely. Such a complete break does not happen suddenly in a healthy relationship, just as a divorce does not occur suddenly in a healthy marriage. It happens only after the relationship has been allowed to cool and deteriorate.

It is inconceivable that a Christian who is truly trying to do what is right and to follow God's will would ever commit a mortal sin. Mortal sin is possible only if we have been gradually backing away from our friendship with the Lord and come to the point where we consider it expendable. Hence, avoiding all sin is the only proper way of life for the Christian, but when we do sin, we should strive to heal the relationship as quickly and as completely as possible. That is the purpose of the sacrament of penance or reconciliation.

c) Knowledge and free will

Many Catholic adults remember that the Baltimore Catechism taught that three conditions must be met for a sin to be mortal: it must be seriously wrong, the person must know it is seriously wrong, and the person must freely choose to do it anyway.

Two things have happened to expand those conditions. One is an increased awareness, fostered by the development of human psychology, of all the factors that can inhibit and limit human freedom of choice. We are more aware today of the many different emotional and psychological factors that can influence our decisions and choices. Thus we are also more aware that the freedom required for a mortal sin, one that completely ruptures our relationship with the Lord, is not to be presumed. Besides those obvious cases of external coercion (e.g., the barrel of a gun in the back), we are aware that many internal pressures can limit the degree of freedom with which we choose an action.

At the same time, if sin is understood in the perspective of a personal relationship of love, it becomes apparent that any sin requires knowledge and freedom, not just mortal sin.

That is why the old lists of sins are less useful today. They are really lists of "wrong" actions, things we should not do. But they only truly become sins when a person's knowledge and freedom are combined with the objectively wrong action. Calling the action itself a sin, without regard to the personal factors involved, fosters the taboo mentality. In the Christian perspective, sin is always a personal reality. Hence lists can be made of actions that are wrong and we can say that such actions, if done with sufficient knowledge and freedom, would be sins. We can even suggest that some actions, because of their serious nature, would normally be mortal sins, but we cannot judge them to be such unless we know the knowledge and degree of freedom of the person involved. Since only God and the person choosing the action can really know that, no one else should even attempt to judge a person's sins. We can judge someone's actions as morally wrong, but we cannot judge his or her guilt.

Even in judging ourselves, determining honestly just what we understood and how free our choice was can be difficult. Awareness of that difficulty has undoubtedly led many Catholics to avoid the sacrament of penance, feeling that they really don't know what to confess anymore. Yet it is not necessary to have precise conclusions about the degree of our guilt in order to be reconciled with the Lord and with the Church. All that is necessary is to throw ourselves on the mercy of God, confess our sins as best we can, and accept the wondrous gift of God's forgiveness mediated by the Church community.

d) Personal and social sin

A final area of development in the contemporary understanding of sin is a growing awareness of social sin. For too long Christian morality has focused almost exclusively on personal, individual sin. The most attention was given to the area that was most personal—sexual sins. In fact, for many people still today, morality is equated with sexual issues. Most Catholics had a somewhat broader view, regularly examining themselves on such issues as lying, stealing, obedience, patience, foul language, skipping prayers, etc. But little attention was paid to those areas of life that entered into the social arena, issues which were part and parcel of the political and social realms and which did not seem subject to the decisions or significant influence of any one individual.

Despite regular and repeated encyclicals from the Popes on social issues, especially since the end of the last century, most Catholics did not consider social issues a matter of sin or a subject for the sacrament of penance. In recent years much more attention is being paid to the moral dimension of political issues, such as corruption, war and peace, justice for the poor, capital punishment, and budget priorities. In the business world, too, questions are being raised about just hiring practices, fair wages, exploitation of Third World countries, corporate responsibilities in plant closings, consumer safety, environmental pollution, and a host of other business decisions that have wide effects on issues beyond the profit figures. People are also increasingly aware of complex moral issues in medical treatment, biological engineering, prolonging the life of the terminally ill, abortion, and organ transplants.

In those and many other issues, the decisions being made involve large numbers of individuals and groups. The issues are complex, and the decision-making process is complex as well. It is difficult to know just what God expects a person to do, and even harder at times to determine who is really responsible for decisions that have been made. It is often easy to determine that sinful decisions are being made and sinful situations are being created, while at the same time it is very difficult to determine how to change what is happening or who is at fault.

Sometimes, of course, the moral issue is clear to a Christian who is in a position of influence in business or government or society and who can make a decision that has significant moral consequences. As Christians recognize that religion must guide decisions in the political and business arenas as well as in personal matters, the question of sin or virtue in such a situation becomes obvious. What is harder to judge is the type of situation in which the political, business, or social system itself fosters injustice or other evils. In those cases the right course may never be as clear as we would wish, yet each Christian has the responsibility to do whatever he or she can to improve the situation and overcome evil.

In that light Christians are becoming more aware of sins of omission in their lives. Sins of commission (acts we have done) are easier to recognize and judge, but often we fail to the live the gospel more by what we do *not* do than by what we actually do wrong. When we pass up opportunities to help others, when we keep silent in discussions in which a moral viewpoint is needed, when we neglect to carry out our responsibility to witness against evil, then we contribute to the sinful situation. While it may be hard to define clearly the extent of our complicity in such situations, certainly our awareness that God calls us to change our behavior in such cases provides a solid basis for confession and forgiveness. We are not fully Christian until we let the gospel influence our decisions and our behavior in every corner of our lives, and much of the conversion of life we need is a matter of properly fulfilling our responsibilities. Sins of omission might be expected to be more frequent matter for the sacrament of penance than sins of commission, especially in the area of social sin.

A Lifetime of Conversion

Understanding the proper place of the sacrament of penance in the normal life of a Christian requires a deeper understanding of conversion than many Catholics have had in past years. Too often we think of conversion as simply a process of joining the Church or changing from one Christian denomination to another. In fact, conversion is a fundamental dynamic of the Christian way of life. There is a role for conversion when one enters the Church, of course. Such a conversion is the basis for the celebration of the sacraments of initiation, as the Rite of Christian Initiation of Adults makes clear. But conversion is not a one-time event; it is an ongoing process. There may be moments of significant change that rightly bear the name of conversion moments, but those moments must be solidified and integrated into one's life.

For most Christians, conversion of life is a slow and long-term process, proceeding day by day and week by week. Step by step we turn our lives over to the Lord and allow God to become truly the center and the focus of our lives. Even if we make a radical decision to turn ourselves over to the Lord, it still takes constant practice to live out that commitment. That is the goal of the whole spiritual life. All our prayer, Scripture reading, celebration of the sacraments, and personal spiritual exercises are directed toward furthering our conversion to the Lord.

When we understand conversion as the fundamental dynamic of the Christian life, penance takes its proper place as an aid to and a celebration of that ongoing conversion. Penance is the sacrament of ongoing conversion, as its patristic title of ''second baptism'' suggests. Only if we are convinced of the importance of constantly seeking to deepen our conversion to the Lord will we discover the vital role that penance can have in our spiritual journey. A Church that is deeply aware of its need for constant conversion will find it both appropriate and necessary to celebrate the sacrament of penance on a regular basis, both rejoicing in the conversion that God is bringing about in its members and also calling every member of the Body of Christ to enter more and more deeply into a converted life in Christ. Penance is not primarily about sin and guilt. It is more basically about conversion and reconciliation, about the grace of God that forgives and transforms us. It is that process of constant growth and change that penance is meant to foster and celebrate.

To understand the sacrament of penance, therefore, is to see our lives as a journey and our faith as a call to change. That may require a deep shift on the part of many Christians who have come to see the Church as the agent of the status quo, the rock of our salvation, the unchanging anchor point of our security. Christ is the anchor and the rock and the basis of our faith, and he is forever the same; but our faith is a call to constant openness to what God has in store for us, and the Christian way of life is a conversion journey that only really ends in heaven. Many fundamentalists are fond of asking, ''Are you saved?'' The proper Christian response is neither ''Yes'' nor ''No,'' for the true follower of the Lord is always being saved by God's grace, but that salvation is not complete until we are face to face with the Lord for all eternity. Penance is the sacrament that celebrates our ongoing salvation through God's forgiving love.

The importance of understanding that conversion dynamic cannot be stressed too greatly. It is the key to understanding much of the renewal of the Church, in addition to being the basic concept of the sacrament of penance. Various commentators have noted that the Church drastically needs a deeper baptismal consciousness, a stronger sense of being called and chosen and set apart as different from the surrounding culture, especially since that ambient culture is increasingly un-christian in its values and priorities and principles. The lack of that baptismal consciousness is rightly seen as the root of many of the pastoral problems the Church faces in the contemporary situation. And such a baptismal consciousness is at root a conversion consciousness, an awareness that the conversion celebrated in the sacraments of initiation is a lifetime journey. Penance finds its proper place as a renewal of baptism and of that baptismal conversion process.

A Reconciling Community

Being more conscious of ourselves as constantly in need of conversion would also tend to make us more of a reconciling community. It is clear from the New Testament, as we have seen, that the Church is supposed to be a community that carries on Christ's work of reconciliation. It cannot effectively proclaim reconciliation to the world unless it is a community that forgives and reconciles readily within itself. As Rev. Harrell Beck commented in a talk some years ago, ''I keep haunting myself with the question: If my little brother or sister is in trouble, will they run *to* the Church or will they run away *from* the Church?'' They will run to the Church if they see that it is a community that is based on and lives by forgiveness, if it is evidently a community that exists to bring about healing and reconciliation. In the struggle to overcome sin and temptation, the Church can easily appear judgmental and even condemning, and if that is the case, people in trouble will surely run the other way.

It should be fairly obvious that becoming more aware of our own need for conversion and forgiveness makes it more difficult to take a condemning or judgmental stance. If we are all sinners, no one has the right to sit in judgment of another. All need God's mercy, and no one really has a superior position. An order of penitents, common penance services, the catechumenate, and solid preaching of the gospel's call to repentance can all help to foster such an awareness within a parish community of faith. The more we recognize who we really are before God, the more we will become a forgiving community that truly welcomes sinners to reconciliation. As Paul admonishes the Ephesians, ''. . . be kind to one another, compassionate, and mutually forgiving, just as God has forgiven you in Christ'' (4:32; see also Col 3:13).

DISCUSSION/REFLECTION QUESTIONS

1. How much of an individualist are you? How community-minded are you?
2. Is our Church truly a reconciling community? Is your parish? Why or why not?
3. What is your personal image of God? Has it changed since you were younger? In what ways?
4. How intimate is your relationship with God? What would help you to increase your closeness to God?
5. Can you think of a time when you reacted to sin as a taboo, an automatic rule-breaking? Have you grown beyond that approach for the most part?
6. Do you operate primarily out of a humanistic understanding of morality, or is the gospel perspective the real basis of your moral life?
7. Has your understanding of penance changed to match your growth in understanding of sin and morality?
8. How helpful is the distinction between mortal and venial sin in your life? How do you determine the difference?
9. Can you imagine yourself committing a mortal sin? How hard or easy do you think it is for the average Christian to do so?
10. What are some ''seriously wrong'' actions you might list today? Some ''less seriously wrong'' actions?

11. What are some things that limit your free will at times?
12. Has your awareness of social sin increased in recent years? If so, what has fostered that? How has your awareness of personal sin changed?
13. How sensitive are you to sins of omission in your life? Do you confess them?

Chapter 6

Getting Practical, or What To Do Till the Parousia Comes

G. K. Chesterton was once asked a favorite parlor question of his time: "If you were stranded on a desert island and could have only one book with you, what book would you choose?"

The great man did not even hesitate before answering, "I would choose Thomas' *Guide to Practical Shipbuilding*."

After reading the last chapter, one might be tempted to despair of ever being able to celebrate penance properly in our lifetime. This sacrament clearly makes most sense and finds it proper setting in a Church with a clear community sense, among people with a healthy intimacy with God and a Christian understanding of sin, as part of a lifetime of conversion in a forgiving and reconciling community. But the Church we know, the parishes to which you and I belong, are far from that ideal. It may take until the Parousia, the Second Coming of Christ, for us to become the kind of community we should be. What do we do in the meantime?

The ideals are important. They give us a direction in which to move and make us aware of the underlying issues that are involved. If those issues are not addressed, efforts to renew the sacrament of penance are doomed to fail.

At the same time, ideals are never fully achieved, so there is no need to wait until some ideal time in some ideal community before we can benefit from those insights into the meaning and value of this sacrament. Whatever the state of our particular faith-community, we can begin by renewing our own perspectives and attitudes. We can seek to deepen our own sense of community and our awareness of our personal need for conversion. We can strive to grow in intimacy with the Lord and to progress in our understanding of sin as a matter of damaging love relationships with God and with the Church. We can open ourselves to the power of the personal encounter within the sacrament and seek out a confessor who offers us such an experience. And we can seek to become reconcilers ourselves, in the daily circumstances of our own lives, to be agents of the reconciliation Christ came to achieve.

A Habit of Forgiving

For many, the best place to begin that ministry of reconciliation is within the family. A Vietnamese folk song suggests, "Hardest of all is to practice the WAY at home, second in the crowd, and third in the pagoda." Whether it is hardest or not, home is where our efforts at reconciliation should begin. Families should be places where forgiveness is freely sought and readily bestowed. Children should be taught from their earliest years that forgiveness is part of loving and living together. Forgiveness is the oil that lubricates the working of the family, lessening the friction that is an inevitable side effect of living together. Whatever our family may be, whether a houseful of children or just a couple sharing life together or an extended family or a religious community, we should strive to make forgiveness a family habit. Those who live alone will find a similar need for continual reconciliation among friends and others with whom life is shared.

Since sacraments are meant to be peak experiences supported by a much larger experience of life, the sacrament of penance will take on deeper meaning to the extent that forgiveness is a reality thoughout our daily lives. Some people seem to have missed that connnection between daily reconciliation and the sacrament, and suggest that reconciling with the person whom one has hurt is a substitute for celebrating the sacrament of penance. They are correct in asserting that penance should not be used as an excuse for not reconciling directly; such seeking and granting of forgiveness should be a normal part of the Christian way of life. But this is not a question of either-or. Direct personal reconciliation does not make the sacrament superfluous or unimportant. Celebrating the sacrament takes the whole process into a broader and richer realm. Our sins never hurt just one person; there are always ripple effects as the one we hurt interacts with others, who thus are affected by our actions (or inactions) indirectly. And the Church community as a whole suffers when we do not fulfill our responsibilities as Christians.

The sacrament of penance encompasses those wider dimensions and at the same time deals explicitly with our relationship with God, which is also affected any time we refuse to love as we ought. Moreover, the sacrament is a celebration that lifts up God's grace, which enables us to forgive and be forgiven, as a cause for rejoicing and praise. Both as individuals and as a community of faith, we need to reflect upon and celebrate what God is doing and what God enables us to do day by day. That is the purpose of the sacraments, and the periodic celebration of penance is a natural outgrowth of our daily experiences of reconciliation.

When to Celebrate

How do we know when it is time to celebrate the sacrament of penance? We have already noted that establishing some kind of schedule by the calendar is not appropriate, since it ignores the dynamics of conversion in one's life. Penance finds its proper place within the spiritual life of the Christian, and celebrating the sacrament makes sense when there is some significant movement of conversion in a person's life. That might be a major shift in a person's life that would lead to entry into the order of penitents for the fullness of sacramental celebration; or it might be a less significant but still notable change of life that might be celebrated in a penance service or an experience of individual reconciliation. In any case, the impetus to celebrate the sacrament of penance should always be a recognition of a call from God to deepen one's conversion or to return to an earlier state of more complete commitment to the Lord.

Describing that call from God is difficult because it takes many different forms for different people and can even be very different from one time to the next in the same person's life. Sometimes it is experienced as a clear sense of guilt over something we have done, with a clear need for forgiveness. Sometimes it is more vague, a sense that things are not quite right with us or a sense of emptiness that makes us ask, "Is that all there is to life?" Sometimes it may be very sudden, as when the death of a friend or a sudden disruption of our life by sickness can make us step back and reflect on where we are heading in life. Or it may be very gradual, as we slowly but steadily become aware that God is asking more of us than we are giving.

Obviously, becoming aware of such a call from the Lord is much more likely if we are attuned to the life of the spirit, taking time regularly for prayer and reflection. Too often we allow the pressures of daily life to eliminate time for prayer and numb us to the promptings of the Holy Spirit. A healthy approach to penance requires a healthy spiritual life. The more we are aware of the Lord in our lives, the more quickly we will recognize God's call to growth and change.

A young boy had been ordered by his father not to swim in the nearby canal, but his father discovered him coming home one evening carrying a wet bathing suit. "Where have you been?" the father asked.

"Swimming in the canal," the boy admitted.

"Didn't I tell you not to swim there?" demanded the father.

"Yes, sir," the boy replied, "but I had my bathing suit with me and I couldn't resist the temptation."

"Why did you take your swimming suit with you?" asked his father.

"So I'd be prepared just in case I was tempted," the boy responded.

Just as we sometimes go to great length to prepare to sin, even more should we prepare well to celebrate the sacrament of penance once we have recognized the God's call to change. Often that will require some time as we sort out clearly, in prayer and/or in discussion with another, just what God is asking of us. That process of discernment is an important part of the dynamics of conversion. Sometimes the recognition of God's demands is hindered precisely by the sinfulness that must be overcome. As we struggle to open ourselves to God's voice, we are already throwing off the domination of sin that has closed our minds and hearts to the Lord. After we have become clear about what God is asking, the struggle continues as we seek to make a decision to change and explore the ramifications of that change in our daily lives.

The process of discernment and change is complex, and it varies often in its shape and progress. For that reason the actual moment of celebration may fit into the process at various points. Sometimes we come to the sacrament knowing that God is calling but still unsure of the dimensions of that call. Celebrating the sacrament often clarifies the issues for us and provides an opportunity to make the decision to change. At other times we may come to the sacrament with the issues clear but with the decision still in abeyance. The celebration can then be an impetus to take the risk of changing and growing. At still other times we may come to the sacrament after the decision has been made and we have begun to live in a new way. In that case the sacrament celebrates the change that has begun and fosters the continuing integration of that conversion in our daily lives.

All of those are valid moments for celebrating the sacrament of penance. In each case the sacrament celebrates the grace of God that calls us from death to life, from sin to holiness, from alienation to reconciliation. The celebration both proclaims and reaffirms the conversion that God is bringing about. It celebrates reconciliation with the Church community and reconciliation with the Lord. Wherever the celebration occurs within the process of conversion, it always provides that peak from which the process can be clarified and fostered.

Celebrating Penance Well

Whenever we celebrate reconciliation, careful attention to each of the three elements of the sacrament can help make it a fruitful celebration. There has been an unfortunate tendency with all of the sacraments in our history to reduce them to the bare minimum necessary. The renewal of the sacraments mandated by the Second Vatican Council requires a deeper experience of the richness of these rituals. That is certainly true of the sacrament of reconciliation, for our recent experience of this sacrament has barely hinted at the richness of its past or its potential for the future. The new rites for the sacrament of reconciliation have been revised to express more of that richness. What remains is that we each renew our own approach to the sacrament in a way that will enable us to experience it more fully and deeply. Attention to each of the elements of the sacrament is one path to that personal enrichment.

Our approach to the confession of sins, for example, would be much improved if we recovered a sense of confession as praise. We confess what God is doing in our lives and how God's grace has called us to conversion. In that atmosphere of praise we share with the confessor where we stand in our relationship with God and the Church. That involves not only admitting our sins but also probing the underlying attitudes and desires that are expressed by our sinful actions. At the same time, a good confession should also include the positive side— expressing how God's grace is being experienced and what growth has been occurring in one's life. In short, our confession should be an expression of where we are on our continual journey of conversion to Christ's way of life.

Making good use of the penance as an element of this sacrament often requires taking it more seriously than in the past. In recent centuries this element has shrunk to a mere vestige of its former self. For many people it has been like a footnote to the sacrament, something to be done in a couple of minutes before leaving church. But the penance can be a vital part of the sacrament, a powerful aid in changing our lives and fostering true conversion. Doing penance really means the hard work of changing the way we think and act and live, and that takes time. The penance we undertake should be practical steps that will make a real change in the way we live. If we have a sense of what would help us change, we might suggest our own penance to our confessor, or we can ask him for guidance. Even if the confessor gives us another, simpler penance, we can always add to that whatever would really help us to change. Taking penance more seriously could help eliminate one of the most common complaints about this sacrament, namely, that it doesn't seem to make any real difference in our lives.

The third element, reconciliation, also needs to be better understood if it is to be appreciated. The first step, perhaps, is to think of it precisely as reconciliation instead of absolution. The word "absolution" speaks of cleansing and a freeing from sin, with a stress on forgiveness. That is certainly an effect of penance, but this sacrament finds its special role in the Church's life precisely in the realm of reconciliation. That is why the revised rites call it the sacrament of reconciliation. The forgiveness of God is available to us in a variety of ways. The sacrament celebrates not only that forgiveness but also the healing of relationships with God and with the community of the Church. In fact, that is the focus of the sacramental symbol itself; reconciliation with the Church is the effective sign of reconciliation with God. That involves forgiveness, of course, but reconciliation is broader and richer, focusing on the relationships that are being healed through God's grace.

When we prepare for the celebration of this sacrament, we need to realize that we are seeking a deeper union both with God and with God's people. Recovering that awareness of reconciliation is perhaps the most important part of renewing this sacrament. Reconciliation is a communal celebration at its deepest core. Its fundamental purpose is to reunite us to the community when we have been separated from it through serious sin and to strengthen our bonds to the community when they have been weakened by lesser sins.

The abandonment of this sacrament by so many in recent years seems to be tied to the realization that God can and will forgive us in many ways, not just through the sacrament. Some people have concluded, therefore, that the sacrament is unnecessary. That conclusion makes sense if we see sin and forgiveness only in individual terms. One can go to God directly and ask forgiveness at any time. But that individualist perspective simply indicates how much we need a deeper sense of identity as a community of God's people. We are saved in community, not in isolation. When we realize how deeply our identity in Christ is bound up with our brothers and sisters in faith, the importance of reconciliation with those brothers and sisters will be obvious and the sacrament of reconciliation will be recognized as a vital part of the ongoing life of the Church and of every Christian.

A Personal Experience

Since the sacrament of penance is a part of a very personal process of conversion, it is clear that the sacrament itself should also be a very personal experience. There are several steps we can take to help make it more personal. The revised rite of penance offers the option of a face-to-face encounter with the priest, an option that many have found to be a very enriching experience, once the initial awkwardness has passed. Those who ignore that option are passing up a prime opportunity to make the sacrament more personal.

Of course, being face-to-face with a confessor with whom we cannot relate doesn't produce a very helpful encounter. The Church has long upheld the right of every penitent to choose his or her own confessor, and we should not hesitate to exercise that right. That should not be a matter of simply avoiding one's own pastor for fear of being recognized. Penance requires more trust than that, and one's own pastor may well be the ideal confessor. But often we may find that we relate more easily and more deeply with another priest, usually because of some unknown factors of personality or style. That does not imply that one priest is necessarily a better confessor (though that may also be true), but simply that different people will find different confessors more or less helpful.

The encounter between confessor and penitent is hard to define, for our spiritual growth and conversion are the issues it addresses, and those realities are complex and involve all aspects of one's life. Many writers have insisted on distinguishing the sacramental encounter from personal counseling and from spiritual direction. While it is true that the sacrament has its own purpose and focus, the encounter between confessor and penitent may often flow from or blend into either counseling or spiritual direction. Both of these dynamics are geared toward fostering personal growth, which is part of the conversion process. What is important is to remember that the sacrament is a moment within the whole process, a moment of celebration and prayer. While spiritual direction and counseling may be part of the larger process and may lead to the celebration of the sacrament, they are not the central purpose or focus of the sacramental encounter. It is a moment of encounter with the Lord within the community of faith and a time of celebrating what God is doing.

On the other hand, spiritual direction or counseling may well be an important part of that larger process of fostering conversion. It may be helpful for a penitent to ask a confessor to spread out the elements of the sacrament over time, similar to the order of penitents but on an individual basis, to allow time for spiritual guidance and working out the penance between the confession and the absolution. Even in a parish that is not experimenting with a full order of penitents, a person can still celebrate the sacrament in this extended form simply by making several appointments with a cooperative confessor.

What is important, however each of us works it out in practice, is that the sacrament be part of that larger process of conversion. If conversion is happening, the sacrament will always find a place in the process. If conversion is not happening, nothing else we can do will make the sacrament come alive.

General Absolution

Many people today are enamored of general absolution as the future of the sacrament of penance. Despite the strict limitations imposed by the Vatican on the use of this third form of the revised rites, many parishes offer penance services with general absolution on a regular basis, and many people participate in those services regularly without ever making an individual confession (which the Vatican requires after general absolution if there is serious sin involved).

While it is certainly possible that we should have more liberal permission to celebrate this form of the sacrament, it is also possible that the popularity of general absolution is an indication of a shallow understanding of reconciliation. Some people seem to seek out general absolution simply because it is easier. When that is the reason for its popularity, it may well indicate an avoidance of the difficult work that conversion requires and may reflect a magical notion of absolution. As long as the magic words are pronounced, the rest of the process is unimportant, so the easiest way to get absolution is very attractive.

Experience with the catechumenate and with the order of penitents has indicated the importance of the personal encounter in fostering the conversion experience. Much care is needed to ensure that any use of general absolution does not short-circuit that process.

At the same time, it should be noted that the history of penance and Vatican II's Constitution on the Liturgy both suggest that a communal celebration of this sacrament is to be preferred over a "quasi-private" celebration. This third form of the revised rites of penance offers the community a way to celebrate God's forgiveness in a truly communal celebration, and it was apparently not intended by those who designed the three rites to be a rarity, used only in extreme emergencies.

Many individuals and community leaders who have experience with a somewhat regular use of general absolution have testified to its potential power to foster true change of heart and honest reconciliation with God and with the community of the Church. That testimony should not be taken lightly, and it is possible that we will see more latitude in the use of this form of celebrating reconciliation in the future.

What is important, ultimately, is not whether general absolution is frequent or rare. What is important is that any and all celebrations of this sacrament be honest expressions of the conversion process that must always undergird the liturgical celebration. Whether the sacrament is celebrated in the form of individual reconciliation, in the context of a penance service with several confessors, in a communal service with general absolution, or in an order of penitents, it should always celebrate the grace of God at work in the lives of God's holy yet sinful people.

Penance and Children

The question of penance for children is one that admits of no simple answers. In recent years the Vatican has tended to insist on introducing children to penance at an early age, ideally in connection with first communion. Many parents and religious educators, on the other hand, have raised serious doubts about a small child's ability to understand and properly celebrate this sacrament. Many confessors can tell true stories of the comical confessions of young children. One second grader confessed that he had committed adultery six times. When the priest asked if he knew what adultery was, the youth replied, "Sure, Father. That's when you disobey an adult."

In light of the understanding of penance presented in this book, it is apparent that any celebration of this sacrament with young children will be an adaptation of the sacrament. The history of penance makes it clear that putting this sacrament before first communion is a rather recent custom. Its celebration with seven-year-olds dates back only to the beginning of the twentieth century, when Pope Pius X lowered the age for first communion, and penance went along for the ride. Penance celebrates reconversion; it presumes a prior conversion that has been celebrated in the three sacraments of initiation (baptism, confirmation, and Eucharist) and makes the most sense only after that initial conversion has been completed and celebrated. In addition, the level of awareness of conversion and God's call to repent and change that the sacrament of penance requires is seldom found in a young child. The process that we have described requires an ability to reflect on one's own life, and that doesn't develop until adolescence at the earliest.

So if penance is celebrated with young children, it must be handled as an adaptation of the sacramental process. Children can understand some dimensions of guilt and sin and change. What is important is that the children are led gradually but clearly into a deepening understanding of conversion and reconciliation. Stress should be put on changing one's behavior, on following the way of Jesus, on becoming a better Christian, and on healing damaged relationships. That emphasis on growth and on reconciliation will provide the basis for understanding penance as the sacrament of conversion as the children become adults.

Perhaps the most important thing we can say about children and the sacrament of penance is that initiation into this sacrament cannot be completed at age seven. Continuing and gradual catechesis is necessary throughout one's formative years if an adult appreciation of this important sacrament is to result.

Conclusion—The Once and Future Sacrament

History teaches us that the sacrament of penance has had a quite varied past. It has varied in form, in place, in frequency, and in style. That history witnesses to the Church's willingness to adapt this sacrament to meet the needs and the spirit of the time. To adapt it has always been possible, but the Church has never been willing to give it up. This sacrament has been too important for the life and growth of true disciples of the Lord.

Many people have begun to wonder if this sacrament has seen its day and should now be left behind. It certainly must be admitted that penance doesn't seem to have much of a present, in contrast to its rich and varied past. Most Christians, including many Catholics, find little or no value in this sacrament today; the majority celebrate it very rarely or not at all.

It would be presumptuous to attempt to spell out the future of penance at this juncture. It seems likely that an order of penitents will play an increasingly important role in that future. Yet it is up to each of us in the Church to discover what the future of this sacrament is for ourselves and for all of us together to determine its future in the Church. May the Spirit guide us all as we seek the best way to make use of this gift of the Lord to the Church.

DISCUSSION/REFLECTION QUESTIONS

1. What is the most helpful ideal that you have discovered in this book? How can you incorporate it into your life?

2. Are you a forgiving person? Do you come from or live in a forgiving family?

3. Do you seek reconciliation directly with those you have hurt? Can you see a role for the sacrament of reconciliation in that context?

4. Is God calling you to conversion at this particular time in your life? In what areas?

5. Have you ever experienced the confession of your sins as an act of praise?

6. How seriously do you take the penance assigned to you in the sacrament? What would make it more effective in helping you change your life?

7. How can we deepen the sense of community and recognition of the need for communal reconciliation in the Church?

8. Do you have a regular confessor? How would you choose one?

9. Have you experienced general absolution? Did the experience foster true conversion in you? Why or why not?

REV. LAWRENCE E. MICK, pastor of St. Rita's Church, Dayton, Ohio, and consultant to the Office for Worship of the Cincinnati Archdiocese, received degrees in philosophy and theology from the Athenaeum of Ohio, and a master's degree in liturgical studies from the University of Notre Dame. He is a member of the North American Academy of Liturgy, the Liturgical Conference, and the North American Forum on the Catechumenate. He has written articles on liturgical topics for *Pastoral Life*, *Today's Parish*, the *New Catholic Encyclopedia*, the *Chicago Catechumenate*, and *Christian Initiation Resources*. His books *To Live as We Worship* (1984) and *Understanding the Sacraments Today* (1987) were also published by The Liturgical Press.